GARLAND
AROUND
MY NECK

© Patwant Singh and Harinder Kaur Sekhon

First Published 2001
Reprint 2019

Price : 500/- PB
Price : 700/- HB

Publishers

B. Chattar Singh Jiwan Singh

Bazar Mai Sewan, Amritsar (India)
Phone (0183) 5011003, 2542346, 2547974
E-mail   : csjssales@hotmail.com
             : csjspurchase@yahoo.com
Visit our Website : www.csjs.com

Follow us on:
www.facebook.com/csjsamritsar

Cover : Dushyant Parasher
Book Design: Dushyant Parasher and Jasvir Singh Garcha

(1000 PB)
(500 HB)

(Printed & bound In India)

Printed by : Thomson Press, Delhi (India)

GARLAND AROUND MY NECK

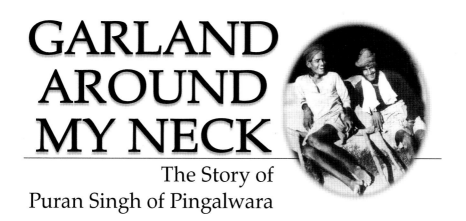

The Story of
Puran Singh of Pingalwara

PATWANT SINGH
and
HARINDER KAUR SEKHON

Publisher

B. Chattar Singh Jiwan Singh

Amritsar

Picture Credits

ਲਖ ਖੁਸੀਆ ਪਾਤਿਸਾਹੀਆ
ਜੇ ਸਤਿਗੁਰੁ ਨਦਰਿ ਕਰੇਇ ॥

Guru Granth Sahib, p. 44

The realm of countless blessings
Is attained by the grace of God

CONTENTS

PREFACE

RECONSTRUCTING the life of the very unusual man who inspired this book was not easy. The long-drawn-out research required endless effort since Bhagat Puran Singh (1904-92) was born at a time when few records were kept of individuals or events – in words or pictures. The practice of keeping written accounts, even of major figures whose destiny was clear from the outset, has never been a strong tradition in India.

The Mughals and the British were exceptions. Their diaries and chronicles show a livelier awareness of the importance of not only documenting the more distinctive features, foibles and characteristics of the men and women of those periods, but a myriad of other occurrences as well without which historians would never have been able to effectively recreate those times. Of course, in order to be remembered, it helps greatly to be born in privileged circumstances; to enjoy all the advantages of birth and heritage, and even more so – for Indians, at least – to be born into the hierarchy of India's caste structure.

Puran Singh had none of these advantages. Nor could he have stood out in those early years as someone whose unique qualities of head and heart would help him establish a new humanistic tradition. And whose compassion and concerns combined with his personal code of conduct and selflessness would make him a legend in his lifetime. So the material on the first forty-three years or so of his life is meagre, and limited to either his own notes, or the recall of people who had known him then, or knew of him. Better documentation is available on events after August 1947 when he returned to Amritsar as a refugee from Pakistan, following India's partition that year.

We were also fortunate to talk to people who had worked with him from that time, till his death in 1992. We met others too who got to know and admire him later, and who supported his life's mission in various ways. The vitality of the oral tradition in India – despite its unrealiability at times – helped fill gaps in the story which would have otherwise remained incomplete.

A rich collection of photographs of the post-partition years proved of immense help in understanding the extent of physical labour he put in to keep his wards fed, clothed, housed and medically treated. These pictures portray the privations he endured without a thought for his own person and with a nonchalance rooted in his amazing stamina and extraordinary willpower. That he was unwilling to invest in even a blanket, a pair of shoes, or a warm garment to help him face Amritsar's bitter winters comes through in stark and uncompromising reality in these photographs. Without this visual evidence of the man's character his life could not have been convincingly documented.

We could not have done better for the title of this book than to use Puran Singh's own words to describe the abandoned, mute, mentally disadvantaged child, crippled for life by a spinal deformity, whom he carried on his back for 14 years. He named him Piara, the beloved one, and described him in his reminiscences as a *garland around my neck*. Piara became a symbol of Puran Singh's caring consistency; of a life dedicated to the uncared segments of Indian society. Not surprisingly, his growing number of admirers gradually began to use the prefix *Bhagat* before his name; a word with sacred connotations which is used for those very few who live exemplary lives inspired by their faith. It was the public's way of paying him homage for his lifelong commitment to his ideals. Whilst a niggardly government scaled down the award one of its own departments had recommended him for, the public recognised the man's unique qualities and offered him the ultimate accolade he so richly deserved.

ACKNOWLEDGEMENTS

THIS book was made possible by the help of those who were generous with their time and whose insights and clarifications proved invaluable. Since photographs feature prominently in this book we would first like to offer our thanks to Deidi von Schaewen who took time off from her always-full calendar of photographic assignments around the world, to take a flight from Paris and motor through Punjab in the hot and humid month of August. The village of Rajewal where Puran Singh was born was the first stop in her punishing travel schedule through Punjab. Her photographs of it, as also her pictures of Pingalwara, add an exciting visual dimension to this book.

The archives of Amritsar's Sewa Studio – where we found photographs of Puran Singh going back to 1951– were of immense help in recreating those early years. The studio's present owner Jasbir Singh told us of his father, Sardar Jawahar Singh's long-term admiration for Bhagat Puran Singh which made him keep a photographic record of his work during those difficult decades.

A chance encounter with Jan Habersatt of Zurich led to his generous gift of some photographs he took of Pingalwara's in-mates. Each one is an exceptional portrait of the men and women who are fortunate enough to battle their inner demons in the caring surroundings of Pingalwara.

Among the many helpful persons whose graphic recollections, personal experiences and unstinting help in our research enabled us to piece together the story of Pingalwara and its founder are J.S. Anand, Prof. Mohinder Singh Bal, Tehmina Bhandari, A.S. Bhatia, Daljit Singh Chadha, Darshan Kaur Chadha, Kartar Singh Duggal, Avinash Kaur Kang, Dr. Inderjit Kaur, Dr. Madanjit Kaur, Dr. Man Singh Nirankari, S.S. Rahi, Pal Singh Rajewalia, Dr. G.S. Randhawa, Dr. Daljit

Singh, Joginder Singh, Giani Mohan Singh, Kirpal Singh, Prof. Pritam Singh, Santokh Singh, Sarab Kalyan Singh, Saran Singh, Sewa Singh and Lt.Col. Thawar Singh (Retd.).

We are indebted to Kartar Singh Duggal for his splendid suggestions with regard to several translations, and for generating such a high degree of enthusiasm for this project in our publisher. The book's design reflects the combined creative talents of Jasvir Singh Garcha and Dushyant Parasher whose imaginative handling of even the minutest design detail can be seen on every page. Parasher's sensitive design of the cover speaks for itself. Antony Wood's editorial advice was, as always, of great help, and it was a pleasure working with J.D. Dewan, an editor *par excellence*.

A special mention is owed to the many staff members of the Pingalwara Society and we are indeed grateful to Dr. Inderjit Kaur, S.S. Rahi and their many colleagues for filling us in on the past and present working of this noble institution.

The confidence with which Anita Mauji coped with the countless drafts of the manuscript merits a special thanks.

This book would never have been written but for the understanding shown by Meher, Maldeep and Rhea, during the two years it took to complete this work. Their spirit of accommodation made it all possible.

January, 2001
New Delhi

Patwant Singh
Harinder Kaur Sekhon

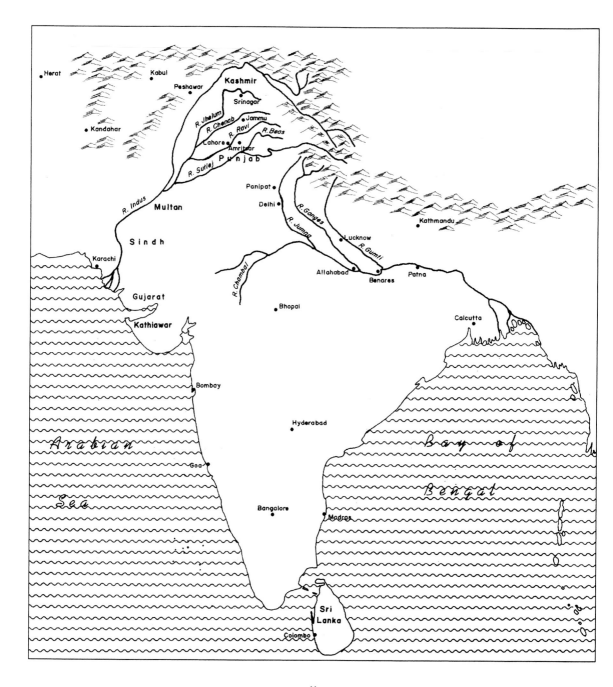

INTRODUCTION

FOR nearly five millennia India has exercised a magnetic attraction on people the world over. Some sailed the seas to trade with her; others came through her northern mountain passes to conquer; still others arrived by caravan. All were drawn by the legends of her exotic religions, faiths and beliefs; her rituals, customs and attitudes; and the lure of her incredible wealth.

Aside from those who came to loot, some, like the nomadic Aryans who descended on India from central Asia fifteen hundred years before Christ, made it their permanent home because of the agricultural promise of its immense flatlands, the irrigation potential of the numerous rivers, the economic opportunities offered by the natural resources and skilled craftsmen. The Aryans mostly preferred the vast northernmost region of latter-day Punjab as an ideal environment for living. But as it straddles the route invading armies from Asia and beyond have traditionally taken into India since then, the distinctiveness of Punjab's inhabitants is rooted in the location of their region. The hordes which periodically laid waste their lands and lives also helped shape the Punjabis' rugged individualism, because adversity engendered in them an amazing fortitude, making them self-assured, confident and prosperous. Punjab's prosperity was not due to great deposits of gold, copper, diamonds and such, but due to the high levels of physical endurance and limitless capacity of its robust people for hard work. Their

adventurous spirit contributed to their reputation as outstanding agriculturists, warriors, travellers and innovators:
qualities, which made them rank among the finest fighting
men in the world, as also sturdy cultivators.

It is a landscape of vast stretches of land traversed by
five rivers – the Jhelum, Chenab, Ravi, Sutlej and Beas – and,
like a great arc to the north the Himalayan ranges which feed
the rivers and send icy winds sweeping across its plains in
winter. Punjab's tough peasantry takes these in its stride just
as it does the searing months of summer, producing – even
more so in recent times – abundant crops of sugarcane, cotton,
wheat, rice, barley, maize, indigo and a wide variety
of fruit. The mix of people – multi-hued, physically striking,
culturally distinctive and religiously diverse – is equally rich:
the men tall, big-boned, muscular, the women light-
skinned, sharp-featured, appealingly audacious with raven-
black hair and luminous eyes.

To balance the prodigious appetites of its hard-working
men – their eating, drinking and merry-making – Punjab also
produces many *sadhus, rishis, bhagats* and *pirs* who preach the
word of God, or sit and meditate on human creation. Still
others practise the essential gospel of religion – service of
humankind.

The successive invasions and colonization of India
introduced new languages, social norms, moral injunctions
and patterns of behaviour. A spinoff of the Aryan migrations
was the caste system, the Aryan language which eventually
evolved into classical Sanskrit, and many other practices and
prejudices, all of which were grafted to the fabric of Indian
life. The entry of Islamic forces into India led to entirely new
social and religious institutions, canons, doctrines, and a
profusion of still more languages and scripts, aside from
great art and architectural masterpieces. So also with two

hundred years of British domination which not only introduced the English language to India, but also their administrative, educational, legal and scientific temper, along with their moral and social precepts. There were other little pockets of European influence too, like the French and Portuguese, with each leaving its own cultural imprint.

India, which has experienced endless wars and bloodshed, brutality and cruelty over several millennia, also provides, paradoxically enough, striking instances of convictions, compassion and self-certainties even when they went against the current climate of arrogance and excess. Such noble exceptions testify to a humane outlook which expressed itself in astonishing contrast to the insular and indifferent attitude of the privileged elites. These exceptional people set an example of selfless and compassionate concern which continues to be honoured centuries later, and legends are constantly retold of the manner in which men shunned the opulent trappings of power to tend to society's lowliest.

Gautama Buddha (563-483 BC), founder of Buddhism, is the most celebrated instance of such convictions. Born to the ruler of Kapilawastu, a small kingdom lying in the Himalayan foothills bordering Nepal, Buddha was brought up in luxury by a doting father (his mother died soon after his birth), and was trained in the art of kingship since that was clearly his destiny. But the meditative side of his sharp and enquiring mind refused to accept that what he saw around him was the sum total of life. Inevitably, despite a beautiful wife, Yasodhara, and an infant son, he renounced everything at the age of twenty-nine to travel incognito and understand the meaning and purpose of the ceaseless cycle of birth, youth, old age, sickness and death. Through practicing self-mortification – ragged clothes, penances,

The three trees planted by Mehtab Kaur

starvation and every other form of self-denial – he learnt a lot about life but not the answers he was looking for. At the end of his tether one day, after six years of unending self-inflictions, he fell into an exhausted sleep under a great tree and when he awoke many hours later, it was to a new conviction, a self-realisation which had eluded him so far.

This tree in Buddh Gaya, in Bihar, under which he found enlightenment, or *bodhi* (wisdom), is since known as the Bodh tree, and Gautama came to be known as Buddha, the Enlightened One. The direction he had to take in life, it was now clear to him, was not the one suggested by other doctrines, but the precepts of a new faith enunciated by him. A faith free of penances, priests, castes and racial prejudices; resting instead on ethical ideals and humanitarian zeal; on equality among human beings, and awareness of the fact that since suffering is caused by desire, controlling desire is the key to an enlightened state of mind. So the next forty-five years of his life were spent on this mission.

While Gautama Buddha did not tend to the poor in the physical sense, by ministering to the needs of the sick and suffering, he lightened their burden of life by opening before them exciting new vistas of human conduct and social justice; by helping create a social environment free of distinctions based on caste and the accident of birth. No wonder Buddhism's appeal spread as far away as China and Japan, and nearer home to Burma, Tibet and other countries in South-east Asia. Ironically, it has almost vanished from the country of its birth after reaching its apogee, because of Hinduism's opposition to faiths which question its 'ordering mechanism' of social and spiritual beliefs.

Despite their hostility towards each other, India's great religions have stressed the importance of humanitarian ideals; of the need to be sensitive towards the suffering of

With Piara – the 'garland' around his neck

fellow-beings. In Hinduism, *dan dharma*, or the principle of giving, is highlighted in various texts from the earliest times. The word *dan* (or *dana*) represents the act of giving voluntarily. In the pre-Vedic period *dan* "was a protection...against starvation for the sick, the aged, the maimed, and the weak, who had the first claim on social property". Even though the manner of giving has undergone changes, the tradition of *dan* continues.

"In Islam, spiritual merit has been assigned to solicitude for the orphaned, the disabled, the victims of circumstances...", and the Quran lays special emphasis on giving. Later theological literature included a detailed table indicating the percentages from different categories of personal wealth which had to be given to the needy. A similar belief has motivated the philanthropic bent of the Parsis. It was enunciated in Persia around 4,000 years ago by their founder Prophet Zarathushtra, and when some of them came to India in the seventh and eighth centuries to escape the Saracenic overthrow of their empire, they kept their founder's injunction very much in mind: "Happiness unto him, who renders happiness unto others."

Almost inevitably the rich religious soil of India witnessed the flowering of another religion whose seed was sown in fifteenth century Punjab by a man called Nanak. Sikhism, the faith founded by him, was an outcome of his quest for philosophical insights into the wars, bloodshed, destruction and other exigencies people experienced in the name of religion. This new faith was a response to the need for correction, for restoring the primacy of humane attitudes, for religious reconciliation and social regeneration after five disruptive centuries prior to Nanak's birth in 1469. The invasions by Mahmud of Ghazni, Muhammed of Ghor,

Tamerlane of Samarkand and others had left in their wake tens of thousands of dead and dying, ransacked cities, and temples looted of their treasures.

Nanak was born in the village of Talwandi near Lahore at a time of comparative calm, between the vicious visit of Tamerlane in the fourteenth century and India's conquest by Babur (founder of the Mughal empire) in the sixteenth. The happy Hindu household in which he arrived as the long-awaited son, consisted of his doting parents and a sister who adored him. Nanak's contemplative mind tried from a young age to make sense of the mutually destructive course on which the great religions of Hinduism and Islam were set, especially because of the disastrous fallout on innocent people. The situation was further aggravated by continuous fighting between Hindu kingdoms and clans, and the bitter battles new Muslim invaders fought with their co-religionists who had colonised parts of the country earlier. Nanak found all this strange, especially since both religions emphasised humane principles: the former through its basic compassion, the latter through its stress on man's essential brotherhood by which all Muslims are equal before God.

Much to his teachers' and parents' dismay he observed very early on that since all human beings – despite different beliefs and persuasions – are equal in the eyes of the divine being, there can be no Hindu and no Muslim. So why did people use religion to repress each other? To find out what men of spiritual stature in centres famous for their religious learning had to say about this, he decided to seek them out – a challenging undertaking given the distances and hazards involved. Leaving home in 1496, his travels – spread over twenty-eight years in all – took him all the way to Mecca, Baghdad, Kabul, Tibet and Ceylon, and in India to Benares, Kamrup (Assam), Jagannath (Orissa) and Hardwar.

Interestingly, Gautama Buddha, who lived 2000 years before him, was twenty-nine when he left home in search of enlightenment, Nanak was twenty-seven. Buddha left behind a young wife and a son, Nanak a wife and two sons. Buddha was a contemporary of Socrates, Nanak of Martin Luther and John Calvin. But there were dissimilarities too. Nanak, unlike Buddha, did not believe in penances and renunciation. Withdrawal from the world was not what he advocated. To him "the secret of religion lay in living in the world without being overcome by it".

At the end of his travels Nanak chose to live in an idyllic spot by the River Ravi near Lahore, a place later known as Kartarpur. Here he gave form to the new faith of Sikhism. A constant stream of people – attracted by his views which were completely at variance with accepted religious beliefs – kept swelling the numbers in the new settlement where life reflected the faith's ideals. People worked side-by-side, whether as tillers, builders, artisans, masons, joiners or just cutting firewood, with Nanak working alongside them to emphasise equality. The concept was further reinforced through the *langar*, or community kitchen, in which men and women, including Nanak, cooked, served, washed up and ate together to overcome existing prejudices which prevented the higher and lower castes from sitting together to eat as equals. No paid helpers are allowed in *langars*. Whilst these symbolic steps stressed the faith's ideals, its moral stand addressed the fate of those who had been pushed beyond the pale of human concern. Nanak viewed equality as a dynamic redressal of stagnant attitudes. To further emphasize their cultural distinctiveness, absolute equality between Sikh men and women was mandatory, with no place for gender prejudices or practices which were discriminatory.

While some saw their God in idols, rituals, customs and

symbols – and different religious groups shed blood to uphold their paramountcy – to Nanak, God represented truth and courage. And He was present in each person. This concept – by which truth attained the status of a Divine Being – became the core of the Sikh faith since he believed that the universality of this idea could help a divided and strife-torn people overcome their prejudices.

After Guru Nanak's death in Kartarpur in 1539, nine others held the office before the tenth, Guru Gobind Singh, decided to end it. (The term *guru* means teacher; it conveys respect for a person's wisdom, integrity, decency and distinctive achievements in his chosen field). Many of the gurus wrote extensively on human conduct; on personal courage and compassion; on the need for rational thought, with the stress always on a positive outlook. The teachings, hymns and verses of the gurus were compiled in book form by the fifth Guru Arjan Dev, and in acknowledgement of the range and depth of Hindu and Muslim thinkers, he included in the anthology the work of men like Namdev, Ravidas, Kabir, Sheikh Farid and others. But Guru Gobind Singh, who gave the final form to this compilation of Sikh scriptures and called it the Guru Granth, went a step further.

In 1708, sensing his end was near, he asked his assembled followers to look to the Granth Sahib as the supreme Guru after him: as the fountain-head of the religion. Placing the mantle of leadership on the Guru Granth was a unique concept which has worked admirably since then. With passages from it read out everyday, it has provided Sikhs with spiritual direction at all times, sustaining them through every travail, strengthening their moral fibre and renewing their sense of purpose. It has become the focal point of Sikh homes, and its tenets have inspired Sikhs through the centuries, just as it moved Puran Singh into undertaking his life's mission.

If it is at all possible to identify a faith's single most important ideal, it would be *sewa* in Sikhism. Not unexpectedly, it shaped Puran Singh's entire outlook as he intuitively understood that although the word means 'to serve', it has a deeper import: a connotation which goes beyond its dry, literal sense. Since God resides in each person, "service rendered to humanity is considered a form of worship and in Sikhism no worship is conceivable without *sewa*". Voluntary *sewa* is a personal commitment enjoined on every man and woman; it seeks no monetary rewards, nor a shortcut to spiritual salvation. According to the scriptures *sewa*, "must be without desire (*nishkam*), guileless (*nishkapat*), in humility (*nimarta*), with purity of intention (*hirda suddh*), with sincerity (*chitlae*) and in utter selflessness (*vichon ap gavae*)". There is yet another, more powerful purpose underlying the idea of *sewa*. "In traditional Indian society work involving corporal labour was considered low and relegated to the humblest castes. By sanctifying it as an honourable religious practice, the Gurus established the dignity of labour – a concept then almost unknown to society."

The Sikh scriptures frequently refer to *sewa*. Guru Arjan Dev prayed for "the pleasure of fanning them [the congregations], drawing water for them, grinding corn for them, and of washing their feet". "Altruism", it is also pointed out, "is the essence of all knowledge." Then again: "He who is turned towards the Guru finds repose and joy in *sewa*." In the annals of twentieth-century Punjab, or in the whole of India for that matter, few brought the range, resoluteness and rigorous self-discipline to the practice of *sewa* as Puran Singh did. A barefoot colossus who strode the century – or at least 88 years of it – he cared for the despairing, disabled and destitute with his own hands, restoring to them the dignity of human existence an uncaring society had denied them.

Puran Singh (1904-92) left a legacy of concern and compassion for not only India's neglected social segments but also for the environment: from the vanishing tree cover to the increasingly polluted air and water. And for animals on whom he lavished the same love as he did on trees and fellow humans. He was quite clear that the existence of each depended on a profound respect for the need to coexist with the others, and just as the founder of his faith committed his life to finding a way out of the mutually destructive religious wars of his time, Puran Singh dedicated himself to dealing with the uncaring and self-destructive course on which those around him had set themselves.

CHAPTER ONE

THE EARLY YEARS

NOT long after the dawn of the last century, Puran Singh was born in very unusual circumstances in the village of Rajewal in Punjab. It was a small village of 500 dwellings, in Ludhiana district of undivided Punjab and off the Malerkotla-Sangrur Road, about 10 miles from Khanna – now Asia's biggest grain market.

Whilst the soil of many parts of the district was fertile, producing fine varieties of wheat, paddy and some rice, it was sandy around Rajewal; more suited to growing maize, millet and lentils which need less fertile land and water. Traditionally, wells and rainfall were the main source of irrigation since the River Sutlej flowed 27 miles away.

The picture changed when major civil works after India's independence in 1947 brought canal waters to much of this region. But a hundred years ago, before modern irrigation facilities became available, farmers found their future inextricably linked with the timely arrival of the rains, and if the monsoon failed they turned to money-lenders for loans to help them tide over the lean periods. Rajewal was well-off because several money-lenders lived there.

Puran Singh was born to one of them on 4 June 1904. His father, Chaudhari Chibu Mal, was a prosperous Hindu of the Khatri sub-caste and his mother, Mehtab Kaur, a Jat Sikh. (Jat does not denote a caste since Sikhism rejects the caste system; the term describes those who are principally, though not exclusively, land cultivators). She was a child widow: a

victim of the vicious custom – widely prevalent in India a century ago – which favoured marrying girls at a young age. More pernicious still was the social stigma attached to widowhood and widow remarriage. So Mehtab Kaur's life was far from happy.

She is said to have been strikingly good-looking and, though unlettered, her interests covered an astonishing range: from love of trees, to animal and bird life, to a compassionate concern for fellow humans. Her concerns developed from her deeply devout nature which made her seek out those who could interpret the Sikh scriptures for her; she also listened to recitations from the great Hindu epics, Mahabharata and Ramayana, at the nearby temple. Increasingly drawn to the service of people and animals, with a growing urge to follow in the footsteps of the ninth Guru and contribute her bit towards the service of mankind, she would spend several hours a day at the village well drawing water for travellers and cattle.

Chibu Mal saw and fell in love with her at this well. He was already married, with a son and daughter. Marriage thus was out of the question for them given the social taboo of widowhood, even though men of means often had two or three wives. What probably happened is that Chibu Mal turned to the practice of *chadar* – still prevalent in present day rural Punjab – to win her over. *Chadar pa layee* is a euphemism for a relationship which falls short of marriage: by placing a shawl, or a *chadar*, on a widow a person (most often a brother-in-law) makes the widow his 'wife'. Perhaps this happened in their case too. In any event in Punjab's male-dominated rural society an affluent man was seldom accountable for his actions.

A strong emotional bond is said to have existed between them even though Chibu Mal imposed a telling condition

A lane in Rajewal >>

on their relationship. He made her promise never to expect a child from him since society would have little time for children born of their union; such children would also represent a transgression of the all-pervasive caste system since they would be offspring of a union between a Hindu Khatri money-lender (enjoying a higher caste status) and a peasant Jat widow (according to him, of a lesser caste). Nor did he want such children to claim his properties years later because these, he said, would belong to the children of his legal marriage.

Mehtab Kaur consented. She had little choice trapped as she had been from childhood in traditional India's constrictive web of casteist prejudices and uncaring attitudes towards the more unfortunate segments of society, especially women. Their lot since centuries had been bedevilled by intolerance, greed, ignorance and the rules of comportment sanctified by time and 'tradition'.

But after three abortions – no doubt at the hands of the village midwife – Mehtab Kaur, unwilling to abort for the fourth time when she found herself pregnant again, pleaded with Chibu Mal not to deny her the right to motherhood. She promised to instill in the child values like selfless service and a commitment to every form of life, and pledged that the child would never ever claim his money or property. Chibu Mal gave in and the son born to them in June 1904 was named Ramji Lal. He was renamed Puran Singh when he converted to Sikhism years later.

The bond between mother and child was incredibly close. She used those early years to explain to him through analogy and personal example, the myriad facets of life around them so that his responses to them would be sensitive and caring. She taught him to pick up all harmful objects like thorns, pieces of broken glass, nails, other sharp objects, stones,

Entrance to Puran Singh's family house in Rajewal >

bricks and such from the lanes and village tracks as they would injure pedestrians, beasts and passersby. "...*itt, rore de utey di jad gadde da pahiya langega ta bailan te ziyada zor paega*". Stones and bricks caused damage to the wheels of bullock-carts – the chief means of conveyance in those days – and a damaged cart wheel meant extra strain on the beast pulling it. Since animals too were living beings, who could not talk, Puran Singh was taught from a young age to be especially responsive to their needs and well-being.

Recalling the deep impression his mother had made on him, Puran Singh narrates how her words and actions stayed with him all his life. He remembers her sending him as a little boy to the roof of their house everyday to feed grains to the birds – the pigeons, doves, crows and sparrows. "My mother would give me a container of corn and ask me to scatter it on the roof...it made me happy to see the birds swoop down for their feed." Her love of trees – which in time influenced his own ecological concerns – had been inspired by accounts of the ninth Sikh Guru Tegh Bahadur's 17th century travels in Assam, in north-east India, where he planted trees in large numbers on the roadside and had huts built to provide shelter for travellers. Puran Singh's mother would tell him that the planting of trees was a great act of kindness since it helps the living environment for a long time to come.

In testimony to her love of trees, the three which she planted in Rajewal almost a hundred years ago still stand majestically though they are now surrounded by water. She planted this 'triveni' of trees (the term triveni means three; in popular mythology it represents the confluence of the rivers Ganga, Yamuna and the mythical Saraswati at Allahabad): a *neem* (*azadrichata indica*), *pipal* (*fycus religiosa*), and *bodh* (*fycus bengalensis*) to provide shade and shelter

Village elders in present-day Rajewal

Jarnail Singh, Rajewal's ex-sarpanch >>

which are highly valued in countries with hot summers like India's. When Puran Singh visited his village decades later in 1981, he had a platform built in his mother's memory around them, but with inundation of the land surrounding the cluster, it is no longer used by villagers or passersby.

An integral part of everyday life in India is the high visibility of holy men who are honoured in the gurdwaras, temples, mosques and other places of worship all over the country, even more so in the countryside where close to seventy-five per cent of Indians live. People give them money and donations of every kind in acknowledgement of the religious role they play in their lives. In keeping with this practice his mother would ask Puran Singh to take either cooked meals or flour to them everyday, and do chores for them as well in the form of *sewa*, or voluntary service. He would also spend time helping his mother at the well drawing water for all who came to slake their thirst, including half the livestock owned by Rajewal's residents.

But through all this there was a deep sadness about Mehtab Kaur, as if she couldn't atone enough, no matter how she tried, for the sin of aborting three lives. Puran Singh intuitively sensed her pain – which she never talked about – and it drew him still closer to her. It is more than likely those early years – and later privations – helped shape his own caring nature and put iron in his spine enabling him to persevere in his life's mission, despite impossible odds.

By all accounts he had a happy childhood. He was dearly loved by both his parents, especially his mother, and on his birthdays free food and gifts were distributed to the poor. The house they lived in was spacious and though the old structure has undergone many changes – including plastering of the original walls – its traditional character still comes through at places. One room, with walls of small-sized bricks and ceiling supported by criss-crossed wooden beams, has been left unchanged. But the room is dilapidated. Renovations to the rest of the house reflect the present owner's preference for the new, instead of old and authentic textures. Nowhere is this more evident than at the main entrance whose massive old wooden doors, carved and ornamented on the outside with nails hammered back into the wood on the inside, have been replaced by a huge iron gate.

In 1916, at the age of twelve, Puran Singh was sent to a boarding school in Khanna – a privileged move for a village lad. He stayed there for seven years, spending his weekends and holidays at home with his mother whose influence on him, if anything, grew with each successive year.

Even now the overall ambience of the village hasn't changed: public sanitation and civic concerns still take a back seat, as they do in most other villages of a Punjab made newly affluent by the Green Revolution from which Sikh farmers emerged as India's biggest suppliers of wheat. So old traditional houses have been replaced by hard concrete structures, with assorted antennae on their roofs and cars, tractors, trucks and jeeps parked in the lanes. Petrol and diesel fumes are now added to the variegated smells from open sewers and garbage heaps which are mostly left untouched. Rajewal village is no exception.

The famine of 1913 foreshadowed the impending tragedy which would soon hit Puran Singh's idyllic existence. Its cause was the failure of rains and it proved disastrous for Rajewal's predominantly agricultural community. For Chibu Mal, despite his wealth, the signs were even more disturbing since he not only stood to lose heavily in his money-lending business, but the failure of crops on his own substantial landholdings was likely to prove equally tragic. Unlike most money-lenders, however, he refused to coerce those who owed him money, and instead travelled north to Lyallpur to buy a railway wagon-load of corn and two wagons of fodder which he sent to Khanna – not for hoarding or selling at a profit but for free distribution to the villagers. He also refused to coerce them to repay their loans until they were able to.

But conditions steadily deteriorated. Erratic monsoons and successive crop failures over the next five to six years drove most cultivators into dire straits. Chibu Mal's money-lending business collapsed as did his agricultural income, reducing this once affluent family to near-poverty. Inevitably, Mehtab Kaur too was badly hit.

But determined to ensure her son's uninterrupted schooling in Khanna without imposing on Chibu Mal in his straitened circumstances, she ground wheat, washed utensils, and did whatever menial work she could get to earn a few rupees each month. "My mother was willing to go to any lengths and undertake any hardship in order to finance my education." Since after a while the village couldn't afford even the meagre sums paid to her for work which took a toll of her energies, she moved to Khanna in the hope of earning more wages, though even there things were no better. Then, in 1919, she accepted an offer from faraway Montgomery (now in Pakistan), almost 300 miles from Khanna, to work for a doctor's family. Mother and son would now be separated for five years, but with an assured salary of ten rupees a month, and free board and lodging, she looked forward to sending a postal money order every month to Puran Singh for his education.

According to his reminiscences his father followed his mother to Montgomery but, being unused to labour of any kind, soon returned to Rajewal. Mehtab Kaur's motivation was different – her son's education was her constant concern and, even more, that he should pass his matriculation examination, which he didn't. Though he fell in line with everything she desired of him, he couldn't get very enthused about his studies and when the time came he failed his exam. It was now 1923. The same year he converted to Sikhism. What happened is explained in his words. "Once, while going to my village on foot, I was forced to spend a night in a Hindu temple, which I voluntarily swept, cleaned and washed, but when it was eating time, the priests dined in my presence without bothering to share even their leavings with me, although they knew that I would have to go to sleep on an empty stomach. As luck would have it, I had to spend another night in similar circumstances at a wayside Sikh gurdwara [Rehru Sahib]. I was a total stranger there and I did not belong to their faith, but I was served a sumptuous meal along with others, which was rounded off with a glass of milk." This experience, he records, "planted in my young mind the seeds of the Sikh faith from which I learnt the lessons of social service, self-sacrifice and the dignity of human life".

His mother had moved to Lahore with the doctor's family that same year, and when Puran Singh joined her there one of the first things she asked him was to again sit for the matriculation examination. On her urging he joined Lahore's Khalsa High School which also admitted him to its hostel.

Lahore has many stirring memories for Sikhs. For long a symbol of Islamic power in Hindustan, it had first fallen to the combined forces of the Sikhs and Marathas in 1758, but the Afghans soon recaptured it until in 1761 the Sikhs retook it. They withdrew after the Afghan governor agreed to an annual tribute and, when he reneged on the payments, they retook it after a swift military action in 1765. But it wasn't till its capture in July 1799 by Maharaja Ranjit Singh, founder of the Sikh Empire, that Afghan power was brought to an end in India. Making Lahore the capital of his rapidly expanding kingdom the liberal Ranjit Singh demanded respect for every mosque, temple, palace and fortress, whether built by Muslims or Hindus. He made equally clear that vandalism of any structure belonging to another faith would be punished and, in his reign, he would not tolerate any discrimination against people of other faiths – an injunction which was fully honoured till his death in 1839.

Amongst the places of historic importance to Sikhs, on which he lavished care was Gurdwara Dera Sahib of Lahore, built in memory of the fifth Sikh Guru, Arjan Dev, who was tortured to death in 1606 on the order of the Mughal Emperor Jahangir. That worthy, resentful of the independent ways of the Sikhs and the extent to which people were drawn to the new faith, was incensed when told – falsely, as it happens – that the Guru was helping the emperor's rebel son Khusru. Primed with hate by his rabid courtiers he had the Guru arrested and done to death. The gurdwara in his memory – opposite the Lahore Fort – was built in the seventeenth century, and was later rebuilt on a more elaborate scale on the orders of Ranjit Singh.

Every gurdwara, the place where Sikhs gather to worship, derives its sanctity from the Guru Granth Sahib, the book containing Sikhism's sacred writings. It is the heart and soul of this house of prayer and devotees are drawn to their gurdwaras because of their serene environs, and because of the inspiration they get by listening to recitations from their holy scriptures. It is a deeply moving and elevating experience and no visit is complete without savouring *karah parshad* – the sacramental food blessed by the Lord and given to every visitor to a gurdwara.

Gurdwara Dera Sahib, Lahore

These places of worship look impeccably clean at all times
as volunteers sweep and wash floors and do whatever else
requires to be done. The ethic of *sewa*, or service, is observed
in many other ways: by ensuring a tremendous flow of funds
for clinics, hospitals, educational institutions, welfare
projects and, of course, new gurdwaras.

As chance would have it, a kindly Sikh's interest after
Puran Singh's arrival in Lahore proved decisive in setting
him on his life's course. The compassionate outlook for all
forms of life around him – which his mother had helped him
cultivate – would now synthesize with the idea of service
through the intervention of Sardar Harnam Singh. This
devout man, owner of Lahore's biggest flour mill and several
other businesses as well, visited Gurdwara Dera Sahib every
morning, walking past Puran Singh's school on the same
street. They took to wishing each other and a tenuous bond
of affection developed between them. Mehtab Kaur too went
to work as a kitchen help in Harnam Singh's household.

It was examination time once again, and Puran Singh
again failed to matriculate. His mother asked Harnam Singh
to place her son in one of his businesses but her employer,
having observed Puran Singh's steadfast and calm
disposition, sensed his potential for other things. He told
her, "*tera put wada aadmi banega...is tohn Satguru ne aapne kam
laine han.*"(Your son will be a big man one day, because God
has a mission for him). On his persuasion Puran Singh took
to performing hours of *sewa* at Dera Sahib every day.

It is quite possibe his own future contribution to society
began to crystallize in him at this stage. He was now twenty,
and the year was 1924. Puran Singh's sensitive nature,
combined with the ideal of *sewa*, was bringing his life's role

into clearer focus. What helped this crystallisation further was that, aside from cleaning, cooking and serving at Dera Sahib, he also tended to the aged, infirm and sick who come to the gurdwaras for help. This caring experience not only made him feel good, it also made him indispensable to Bhai Teja Singh, the head of Dera Sahib.

The place became his home for the next twenty-three years (although some time out of this was spent at Lahore's Gurdwara Shahid Ganj and at Amritsar). During this period he indulged his other great love – libraries. These storehouses of knowledge, with their immense scope for improving his mind, fascinated him as he was constantly searching for answers to the many philosophical, humanitarian and environmental questions that intrigued him. His favourites were the Dyal Singh Library and Lala Lajpat Rai's Dwarka Das Library, although he visited others too in Lahore. The works he read ranged from John Ruskin, Emerson, Tyson and Thoreau to Mahatma Gandhi. Equally eclectic was the variety of journals he read, finding Gandhi's weekly, *Young India*, of particular interest. "From it I learnt that the colonial rulers of India, by their economic policies, have ruined the traditional village economy of rural India where more than 80 per cent of people live." He was struck by the argument that self-help was the only way out, whether through the revival of traditional crafts and skills, or in countless other ways. In all likelihood his reading habits provided the impetus to his own future endeavours.

On another level, Puran Singh reveals in his writings an incident which left a profound impression on him in 1925. An old man, with a badly infected leg, limped into the gurdwara one day. Puran Singh, on seeing maggots oozing out of a very small hole in his calf, took him to Lahore's Mayo Hospital – the biggest in undivided Punjab. The ailing man was admitted and given a proper bed with clean sheets to sleep on. At this he gratefully remarked: "I know I am going to die soon. But at least here I will die in peace and comfort." To Puran Singh this brought home the fact that it was everyone's right to die with dignity when the end came and there was little else left to look forward to.

This period of grace – which was about to end – gave him a sense of purpose, and a resoluteness which would help him through the troubled times ahead. In 1929 his mother fell ill and expressed a wish to visit Rajewal for the last time. Puran Singh took her there though neither was prepared for the shock which awaited them. Chibu Mal had died a few years earlier and his property now belonged to his son, who flatly refused them permission to stay in his house. Others in the village behaved no better, so Mehtab Kaur suggested they go to Amritsar, the fountainhead of the Sikh faith.

It was a difficult existence. Apart from a brief spell in Tarn Taran – another Sikh pilgrimage centre – they lived on the road near the temple, amongst beggars and such. From here they moved to a vacant lot near a gurdwara at a place called Chheharta and lived in a makeshift hut Puran Singh built for them. They ate in the *langar* where he spent most of his time doing *sewa*. He would also go, whenever possible, to Amritsar's Guru Ram Das Library.

Mehtab Kaur was now extremely frail. Knowing her end was near she confessed to her son she had never legally married Chibu Mal and had had three abortions, the third of which was carried out when the foetus was fully formed. Time had not lessened her pain, nor sense of remorse at her "misdeeds", and all of Puran Singh's efforts to convince her that she was blameless, and it was his father who had forced her into doing what she did, could not lessen her sense of guilt. He said he would always honour her confidence in him, and promised to live the life of an ascetic, unattached to all material things; to better dedicate himself to caring for the destitute, he promised to remain a celibate all his life. He also vowed never to make any living being suffer. She died in his arms, on 23 June 1930, while he was still reassuring her.

Puran Singh's writings reflect the enormity of his grief, the feeling of utter emptiness at her death. He was too benumbed to even weep, for the loneliness which engulfed him was indescribable – the feeling that he had no one in the world he could call his own. But he was determined not to let despair deflect him from his pledge to his mother. And equally determined to become a rallying point for those worse off than him.

CHAPTER TWO

THE TURNING POINT

THE turning point in his life came in 1934. And it came without fuss or fanfare. He had returned to Lahore and Gurdwara Dera Sahib after his mother's death – to immerse himself again in his old routine of *sewa* and studies – when in November that year he came upon a child abandoned near the main gate of the shrine. The boy was about four years old. Dumb, mentally impaired and physically deformed, he was suffering from acute dysentery and was covered with flies and his own faeces. Puran Singh, given the responsibility by Giani Achhar Singh, new head of Gurdwara Dera Sahib, of looking after the child, washed and fed him and named him Piara, or the loved one. From that day on they were inseparable for the next 14 years (until 1948, when he had assembled a group of those, discarded like Piara, with whom he could leave him for a few hours at a time). "The act of carrying Piara Singh on his back [became] symbolic of his carrying all...the aged, the infirm, the disabled, the crippled, and the sick, on his shoulders." It was not easy since the helpless boy's hands and feet were lifeless, and he would constantly drool on Puran Singh.

More even than the recipient of his love, Piara became the *raison d'etre* for Puran Singh's mission in life. Space at Dera Sahib had always been a problem, even though with his customary ingenuity he managed to find a solution. He first created a cycle stand for the hundreds of people who stopped by to visit the shrine every day. Their cycles would

< A view of Gurdwara Dera Sahib from the Sheesh Mahal, Lahore Fort

be piled haphazardly until Puran Singh, using simple materials like bamboo sticks, cane and rope, laid out spaces which made parking of cycles much easier. Using the same materials, plus some matting, he then built a small hut at one end of it for Piara Singh and himself. But since space was still restricted Puran Singh partially moved to Shahid Ganj whose added attraction – aside from its large area – was the number of impaired and infirm sheltered there who needed looking after. Knowing the space would do Piara good he moved to the basement of this gurdwara built by Maharaja Ranjit Singh to honour Sikh martyrs who died fighting the Mughals and Afghans in the 17th and 18th centuries. Foremost among them was Bhai Mani Singh, a scholar and lifelong confidant of Guru Gobind Singh, the tenth and last Sikh guru who founded the Khalsa in 1699. Mani Singh's execution was ordered by Zakariya Khan, Lahore's Mughal governor, and Sikhs hold this memorial in great esteem. For Puran Singh it was an elevating environment in which to tend the sick and suffering.

In the countdown to India's partition in 1947, twenty men, women and children lived there and though some volunteers did help, Puran Singh laboured from early dawn to late at night to keep them fed, bathed, clothed and medically treated. When not tending them he was out on the streets of Lahore, trying to raise money for his mission. "A tall, shabbily dressed man...tramping with his wooden sandals, or riding a rickshaw along with an invalid, he always carried a brass-bell hanging by his side and announcing his arrival."

But bloody events would soon shatter the calm of this peaceable existence, uprooting millions from their traditional homes, lands and livelihood, while hundreds of thousands would lose their lives because of the cynical decisions taken by Indian politicians and the British who then ruled India.

Independence from the British was something Indians of all religious beliefs and ideologies had dreamt of ever since the struggle for self-rule began decades ago. But what the vast majority of people had no inkling of was the price they would have to pay for getting their independence. That price would be the Indian subcontinent's partition along religious lines, with the Islamic state of Pakistan on one side, and a secular India on the other.

The staggering toll of partition in terms of lives lost was borne by Punjab, since those who agreed to divide India – in the manner in which they did – showed a marked preference for political expediency and not a principled approach to a problem which concerned millions of Punjabis and their future. By agreeing to the transfer of populations as the basis of partition, the three signatories to the plan – the Congress Party, Muslim League and the British – sealed the fate of those who would become minorities overnight on either side of the new border, and who would be forced to move to where their co-religionists were the dominant community. This is what did happen, once the three took the decision to divide the country. Frenzied mobs were encouraged to forcibly expropriate the properties, wealth and lands of affluent Sikhs and Hindus in places which would soon become a part of Pakistan. Violence against them first exploded in Rawalpindi, a predominantly Muslim city, five months before 15 August, 1947 – the date agreed upon for partition. It took another month after this date for the same murderous violence to break out on the Indian side of the border with Pakistan. In all partition took over 600,000 lives and uprooted fourteen million Sikhs, Hindus and Muslims from their homes and the familiar surroundings which had nurtured them for generations. This was the price paid for a perverse political decision.

The extraordinary scale of the blood-letting is all the more tragic since the three major religious communities – the Hindus, Muslims and Sikhs – had celebrated their festivals, *Basant, Baisakhi* and *Lohri* with as much gusto as their religious festivals like *Gurpurbs, Id, Diwali* and *Dussehra,* and dressed for the occasion in exuberant and festive colours. The places they worshipped in – the Sikhs in *gurdwaras,* Hindus in *mandirs* and Muslims in *masjids* – dotted Punjab's landscape, whilst the lyrics sung to legendary lovers like Heer-Ranjha, Sohni-Mahiwal and Mirza-Sahiban filled the air in the evenings.

The brutal events of partition ended this phase. As city after city in West Punjab (soon to become a part of Pakistan) exploded in blind sectarian violence, erstwhile friends and neighbours turned on each other with hate fanned by power-hungry politicians and religious fanatics. Lahore was no exception. Muslims, who were in a majority, took to the streets in murderous fury attacking even Gurdwara Shahid Ganj on 13 August, 1947. Puran Singh and Piara escaped because they were in Dera Sahib that day, but a volunteer working in the gurdwara was slaughtered. Three days earlier another person who helped him look after the inmates, and fetched food from Dera Sahib's *langar* twice a day, had been arrested for violating the curfew whilst returning to Shahid Ganj; Puran Singh never saw him again.

India's partition was Lahore's swan song. This colourful and cosmopolitan city in which Hindus, Sikhs, Muslims and Christians had invested a great deal of emotional capital and left their imprint on its culture and character; where they lived together in a spirit of bonhomie and good-natured bluster; whose bazaars, lanes, boulevards and eating places reflected the vitality, energy and elan of men and women of different races, religions and beliefs was destroyed overnight by the braying intolerance of religious bigots. Lahore's rich texture of the wealthy and westernised elites, hedonists and ascetics, students from its many centres of learning, prosperous hoteliers, merchants, traders and restaurant-keepers, and the entire range of faiths from the formal to the mystical sufis, vanished forever during the dark days of partition. The city lost its soul due to the mindless folly of those who had happily coexisted in its embrace yet in the end allowed religious intolerance to destroy their inherent sensitivities.

On 18 August with the fate of his luckless fellow-workers and wards weighing heavily on him, the forty-three year old Puran Singh climbed on to a refugee-laden truck headed for the safety of Amritsar. He had a little over a rupee in his pocket and a crippled and mentally deficient boy of seventeen on his back. He was just one among several million refugees who would cross the border to reach India during those traumatic days of murder and mayhem. Puran Singh had no family in India, nor friends, acquaintances or kinfolk to whom he could turn for help. He was unsuited by inclination and temperament to ask for help anyway, although he himself had always reached out to help the disabled, ill and despairing. The crippled boy on his back, Piara Singh, was one such. When he arrived in Amritsar on that sweltering day in August 1947, he had looked after Piara Singh for thirteen years; from the day he had found him on the sidewalk covered with flies and his own body-wastes. He had fed, cleaned, washed and cared for him ever since, carrying him wherever he went since he had no one to leave him with. In his reminiscences Puran Singh describes him as a "garland around my neck".

Writing of that period in Lahore, a former judge recalls "the year 1940 when he [Puran Singh] walked barefoot and half-naked on the roads of Lahore, usually with a crippled boy as a sacred load on his back...." A former vice chancellor

Puran Singh and Des Raj who lent him a helping hand on 18 August 1947

Khalsa College, Amritsar

of Punjab University remembers that "for fourteen years, well before the inception of his institution [Pingalwara] he had to carry the crippled boy...undergoing not only great physical strain but also...the ridicule of people".

Which well-spring did he draw upon for his endurance and compassion, for the strength with which he faced the recurring tragedies in his life? "Whatever the work, my willingness to undertake it has always been due to my implicit faith in God...if it meant getting my hands dirty, so be it...it was God's work." Born in a region which prides itself on the military prowess of its men, Puran Singh's steadfastness and unflinching courage in adversities – though of a different order – were no less remarkable.

Ninety year old Des Raj who extended his hand to help Puran Singh get down from the truck in Amritsar on 18 August, 1947, can still recall that day: "There was something striking about this tall, gaunt man cradling a cripple in his arms, wrapped in a *chaddar* and wearing only a *kachh* (knee-length underpants), with *kharawan* (wooden sandals) on his feet." Puran Singh's records show that he also brought with him "from Lahore a man who was on his deathbed and who died within a week of reaching Amritsar". It is unclear whether the man had been abandoned by his family and Puran Singh had taken charge of him, or whether he had come with him from Lahore.

Amrik Singh Bhatia, then aged ten, who had arrived in the camp just hours earlier and witnessed the encounter between Des Raj and Puran Singh – destined to become friends and colleagues in the years ahead – also remembers that day well. Des Raj was a medical dispenser in the army on loan to the camp established in Amritsar's Khalsa College for taking care of the refugees who were streaming across the border barely sixteen miles away. Piara and his mentor were two amongst 25,000 or more admitted to the camp. The suffering Puran Singh saw there exceeded anything he had witnessed before. Many of the men, women and children were separated from their families in this great exodus with the ailing and aged, often abandoned, somehow finding their way to the overcrowded camp which – with its limited space and resources, and hot and humid weather – was soon in the grip of gastro-enteritis and cholera epidemics. To Puran Singh these conditions posed a personal challenge.

Khalsa College, a venerable institution founded in 1892, was headed during those trying days by Bhai Jodh Singh, a distinguished educationist, who was its principal from 1936 to 1952. Appointed camp commandant to deal with the refugee crisis, he struck Puran Singh as a humane man who, given the meagre resources available to him, was stretching himself to the limit to help the stricken and uprooted refugees who had completely overrun his orderly and well-tended campus. Jodh Singh was equally impressed by this odd-looking, self-confident stranger who willingly got down to any kind of work. They soon established a good rapport.

Puran Singh's prime concern became the sick and handicapped who were unable to fend for themselves and whose problem was further aggravated by a poorly functioning kitchen where a near-stampede occured at meal times with the disabled unable to get near the food. Puran Singh took to fetching it for them twice a day despite the problem of where to leave Piara in that crowded camp. An incontinent and mentally disadvantaged person was not always viewed kindly by people. Piara, though seventeen, could not sit up by himself due to a spinal deformity, so Puran Singh carried him on his back on most of his errands; he also had to give him an enema everyday. He writes that his faith in God and the impetus provided by Piara helped

him overcome all odds. "Piara has been the greatest source of strength and inspiration for me. But for him, I would not have been able to achieve whatever I did in the form of Pingalwara."

The feeding of those in his care was only one aspect of the problem. He had to get medication for the sick and arrange hospitalisation for the more serious cases as well. Neither task was easy in the prevailing conditions. The situation worsened with the epidemics; patients suffering from acute diarrhoea and cholera were unable to ingest the food served by the camp's kitchen and to buy fruit and yogurt for them would cost three rupees a day, which Puran Singh did not have.

Though he kept managing, an incident provides an insight into those times. A seriously ill refugee, who usually lay under a tree, one day gave Puran Singh some money to buy him a cold drink. After he had fetched it he asked the man if he could spare some money for others less fortunate. The man pretended not to hear. Puran Singh continued to care for him but found him dead the morning of the third day after the incident. Convinced that the dead man had at least thirty or forty rupees on him, he debated whether to search him and keep the money for his patients, or hand over whatever he found to the camp authorities. He neither wanted to be branded a criminal nor forego this chance to help his disabled patients. When he did put his hands in the man's pockets he found Rs. 1710 – far more than he had ever imagined.

Puran Singh picked up the corpse, and then another of a woman lying close by who had also died in the night, and arranged for their cremation which cost him forty rupees. Out of the Rs.1670 left, he spent some on his wards during the next few days but as his conscience kept disturbing him,

< With two of his crippled but happy wards

he finally sent the money to the family of the volunteer worker who was killed at Gurdwara Shahid Ganj in Lahore, and whose wife and children had managed to reach India and were trying to rebuild their lives in Kanpur.

That Puran Singh's sensibility was vastly different from others, and not many would have made the choices he did, became evident in other ways as well – like when, at the height of the gastro-enteritis and cholera epidemics, he would collect the soiled clothes of patients and wash them every day. He had become friends with Shambu Nath, owner of a factory across the road from Khalsa College which had the facilities Puran Singh needed to wash his pile of dirty clothes. An electric pump in the factory fed water under high pressure to an overhead tank which would then supply it to four taps at the ground level with great force. This would enable him to easily and expeditiously remove the filth in the clothes he brought for washing everyday.

Years later, Principal Jodh Singh, in recollecting those days, wrote: "Washing filthy clothes with his hands, and keeping the bodies of his helpless patients also clean were tasks which most people would feel squeamish about but which Puran Singh took in his stride." Witnesses who are still around recall with amazement the seemingly limitless stamina of the man and his levels of physical endurance which drove him around the clock. At age forty-three he was – no doubt subconsciously – conditioning himself for the demands of the even more gruelling pace which awaited him over the next forty-five years of his life.

The refugee camp at Khalsa College was wound up on 31 December, 1947. Most of its inmates were dispersed to start life afresh wherever they could, though there was complete uncertainity about the future of the incapacitated and mentally unstable. Puran Singh had looked after twenty or so of these, including five children, and he decided to take with him those who had nowhere else to go. He had no idea where he would take them, but the thought of abandoning them never entered his mind.

Puran Singh was absolutely certain that Amritsar was where he wanted to be. He was keen to establish a home in the city for those whom an indifferent and self-indulgent society had overlooked. His decision was based on sound reasoning. As the holy city of the Sikhs where the supreme emblem of their faith – the Darbar Sahib (the Golden Temple) – is located, Amritsar exercises a magnetic pull on them. Thousands come around the year to visit it and Puran Singh intuitively understood how valuable their support could prove if they saw for themselves what he was trying to achieve, especially since the ethic of community service is integral to the Sikh faith.

The site where the city of Amritsar is built was selected for meditation and prayer by the third Guru Amar Das (1552-74). He was struck by its beautiful location alongside a tranquil stretch of water in a forested terrain. It lay about 35 miles east of Lahore. His successor Guru Ram Das (1574-81) saw its potential as a pilgrimage centre, a place where Sikhs could come for inspiration and renewal. Its eventual design took the form of a serene structure in the centre of the pool – the immortal pool, as the Sikhs call it – the four sides of which became the *parkarma*, or circumambulation, around which devotees walk before crossing the causeway that takes them to the Harmandir in the middle of the pool.

The foundation stone of this most exalted of all buildings in the Darbar Sahib complex was laid in 1588 during the fifth Guru Arjan Dev's (1581-1606) stewardship. The name Amritsar evolved from *amrit sarowar*; *amrit* is water sanctified

Darbar Sahib

by the touch of the sacred, and *sarowar* is the word for pool. The city of Amritsar grew around the shrine in the pool.

Determined to do his life's work in Amritsar, Puran Singh, after leaving Khalsa College, first moved his group under a large *pipal* tree by the roadside, near the railway station. With its generous spread and luxuriant foliage of shiny green leaves, the *pipal* is a familiar sight on the Indian landscape, providing a roof to those without one, and welcome shade from the scorching sun to passersby. But if the summers are hot, winters in the north are equally cold, especially from December till February when there is frost on the ground at night, and the chill pierces the body. So Puran Singh moved a few of his wards under an arch designed to carry a staircase from the ground to the first floor of the railway post office. Not a very wide arch to begin with, it was bricked on one side and thus provided only a narrow strip of space under it. But it was a shelter of sorts anyway for some of his wards. Others were placed in a not-too-frequently used toilet block attached to the same post office, and still others in the tin shed of the nearby tonga stand. The former was smelly and unhygienic but preferable to being out in the bitterly cold night, and the latter too, though it had its drawbacks, was open and airy. Two tonga owners, Bachan Singh and Hira Singh, remember Puran Singh with admiration and affection, and speak of his compassion for humans and animals alike.

Puran Singh then took everyone under his care to the compound of the railway station. This took nerve, but he had plenty of it. He was in no mood to let frowning railway officials affect his resolve because the advantages of this location were immense: he could take the sick to the nearby Victoria Jubilee Hospital (later renamed Guru Tegh Bahadur

Space under this arch was also used as a shelter for his wards

< Pipal tree opposite the Amritsar railway station

Tonga stand outside the Amritsar railway station

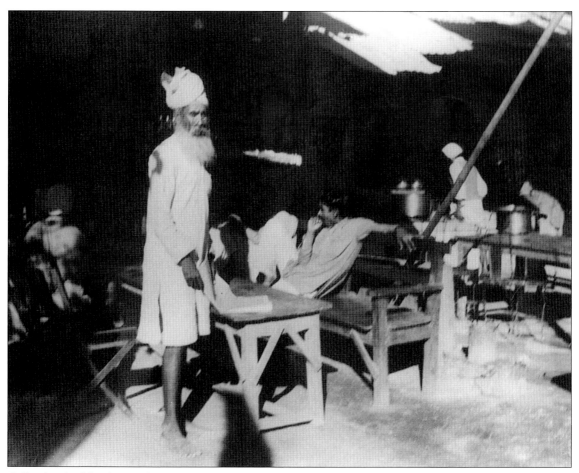

Collecting food for those in his care

Hospital); he could collect food everyday for his patients from the not-too-distant residential areas, and also from the many *dhabas* (eating places) outside the railway station.

Another advantage outweighed all others. Since trains were the preferred means of communication in those days the number of people who would see what the city's neglected segments were up against would greatly help his cause. If he attracted the attention of those in privileged positions who used the station all the time, he could interest them in helping him build a permanent home for the helpless. This reasoning worked. And before Puran Singh moved out of Amritsar's railway station on 1 October, 1948, a number of influential politicians, philanthropists and others had taken note of his mission. Though large-scale help was still years away, voluntary donations from Sikhs started coming in and, to him, this broader base of support was more satisfying. There were some who found this strange looking, unkempt man an oddity and his work unconvincing. "Sometimes his mission appeared quite implausible," says Dr Daljit Singh, Amritsar's distinguished and widely admired eye surgeon. His recollection of Puran Singh goes back to 1951, when he was a student in the medical college, but his early scepticism gave way to a lasting respect for this unusual man. "No one had his missionary zeal."

Puran Singh established his next camp under a huge and heavily foliaged *bodh* tree opposite the Guru Tegh Bahadur Hospital. The site was spacious, the air fresher, and medical aid was within easy reach. It was close to Company Bagh, a sprawling garden-park which would help the mentally handicapped observe different forms of nature around them. But by the end of 1948 he had to move again. The timing couldn't have been worse as it was terribly cold. Unfazed,

Puran Singh soon found an abandoned house nearby, opposite the office of a senior district official, the civil surgeon. He promptly moved his expanding flock into this dilapidated structure, and even though one of the rooms had no roof, it was 'home'.

Puran Singh's mettle was once again tested in this new location after his encounter with a woman by the name of Asha Rani and her four year old son Jeeta. She was suffering from advanced tuberculosis and too weak to take care of herself and her son; her lungs were so severely damaged even breathing was a major effort for her. Seeing her condition Puran Singh asked the doctors at Guru Tegh Bahadur Hospital to persuade the TB Hospital to admit her, but it had no facilities for in-patients. Undeterred, he took her in his charge and, to segregate her and prevent others from getting infected, kept her under the ornate structure of the nearby Maharaja Ranjit Singh Memorial Gate, which was close enough for him to look after her. Knowing death was imminent, he did everything to make her feel part of a family in the last days of her life. He told her she should not worry about her son Jeeta, that he would always be looked after. Puran Singh's heart went out to the little boy with the air of a grown-up's strong sense of responsibilty towards his ailing mother, but also the innocent's look of infinite sadness. And all this at the age of four! Within two weeks Asha Rani was dead. Puran Singh reverently cremated her, but before that had a woman bathe the body in keeping with religious beliefs. Jeeta survived his mother by only a few months and died of the tuberculosis he had contracted from her. In the brief period of life left to him he would cling to Puran Singh all the time, refusing to sleep without him. Puran Singh, not wishing to add to the boy's unhappiness, would cover his own nose and mouth with a wrap to reduce his chances of infection.

Ranjit Singh Memorial Gate, Amritsar

< With the orphan, Jeeta

A little more than a year later, by 1950, he had to move again because the local administration wanted the house he was in vacated as it was illegally occupied. Its inmates had by now risen to sixty. Puran Singh next set his sight on an unfinished and abandoned cinema hall whose owner Feroze Din, a rich Muslim, had migrated to Pakistan. Seeing it would suit his needs admirably he promptly moved into it, and inevitably the count of the destitute and disabled also increased. True to his custom he looked after his wards' needs personally, avoiding dependence on others for the countless big and small jobs to be done daily. But his mission was attracting volunteers, and one of the first was Des Raj who had helped him alight from the truck the day he had arrived from Pakistan. The combination of Des Raj's experience as an army compounder, his work in the refugee camp and his caring nature, worked well with Puran Singh's own chemistry. Joining him in 1948, Des Raj stayed till 1987, the year he retired as general manager of Pingalwara. Privy to all major decisions, he made a lasting contribution to its growth and, according to him, it was he who suggested the site for Pingalwara when he and Puran Singh were walking past it one day. An open stretch of land diagonally across the road from Amritsar's main bus-stand, both its location and Des Raj's impromptu remark appealed to Puran Singh and when the government did offer him land he chose this.

A year after he moved into the incomplete cinema, Puran Singh took over an abandoned mosque close to where the future complex of his institution would be built. After witnessing Asha Rani's tragic fate, and given the number of people in India who suffer from TB, he planned to use the mosque for the exclusive use of patients afflicted with tuberculosis and other communicable diseases. Now known as the Piara Singh Ward, it presently houses over a hundred male patients. The progressive and well-educated Executive Officer of the Amritsar Municipal Committee, Padam Chand Bhandari, graduate of Cambridge University's Corpus Christi College who had done his Bar-at-Law from the UK, impressed by Puran Singh's initiative and efforts, offered to add five rooms to the TB annexe, which he later increased to eight. His widow Tahmina Bhandari, now 92, who did her MA from Khalsa College in 1936, also gave Rs.10,000 to Bhagat Puran Singh for his 'mission', as she put it.

The cinema hall became his 'headquarters' for the next seven years, providing a welcome respite from his all-too-frequent moves. Even as the numbers of those in his care increased, so did appreciation of what he was trying to accomplish. In 1951, Gopi Chand Bhargava, Punjab's Chief Minister, who had observed Puran Singh's work for some years, requested the Union Minister of Rehabilitation, Mehar Chand Khanna, to sanction a piece of land for him, as a result of which he was given possession of the plot near the bus stand on the Grand Trunk Road. Valued at Rs. 40,000, the main complex of Pingalwara would be built on it, but since there was no money to start construction, Puran Singh continued to operate from the cinema hall till 1957. Although sympathisers tried to buy this property for him when it came up for auction that year, they were unsuccessful, and its new owners soon had the inmates evicted. Philanthropy was not on their agenda.

Puran Singh now brought his wards to an old, unused building in the Ram Talai area – also on Amritsar's Grand Trunk Road. It belonged to a charitable foundation, the Rai Bahadur Kalyan Singh Memorial Trust, named after the man who had brought the tea trade to Amritsar in 1830. Fortunately for Puran Singh, the trustees reacted more compassionately to his occupation of their property in view

Early makeshift shelters at Pingalwara >>

A Pingalwara inmate

of his perseverance and commitment, and though some differences did develop, the building has stayed with Puran Singh and his successors ever since. With another more or less permanent place he could now depend upon, the future form of Pingalwara started to take shape. (The Trust's building was named the Ram Talai Ward and, after Puran Singh's death in 1992, it was renamed the Mehtab Kaur Ward in memory of his mother. It houses around 180 women patients suffering from epilepsy and various mental disorders.)

A word about the Grand Trunk Road – India's oldest and most historic highway. It was built by Sher Shah Suri who in 1540 defeated and forced the second Mughal Emperor Humayun to flee the country, and whose own brief rule extended over large parts of India. The road originated at Sonargaon (now in Bangladesh) and extended all the way to the River Indus (now in Pakistan), linking along the way some of Hindustan's major centres including northern cities like Agra, Delhi and Lahore. After the Sikhs founded Amritsar in the 16th-17th century, the city became an important generator of commercial traffic on this highway – known as *Sarak-e-Azam* in Suri's life time.

On 6 March, 1957 the All India Pingalwara Society was duly registered with the government. What does Pingalwara mean? The word is interpreted in several ways. To some it means a 'home for the crippled', to others a 'home of lepers'. Still others prefer to call it a 'home for the handicapped'. Its literal meaning aside, what it represents for countless people is an institution where the terminally ill, mentally challenged, crippled and abandoned are fed, tended, treated and cared for. By now it is not only a household word in Punjab, but because of the Sikh diaspora is also known around the world, proof of the fact that word-of-mouth publicity can

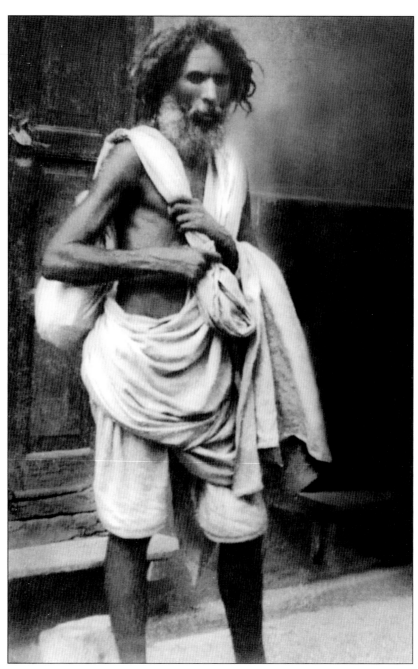

His personal appearance was unimportant to him

achieve a great deal. This proved especially helpful for Pingalwara which had no capital other than its founder's unbending will and dedicated labour. Some people feel the name Pingalwara does not convey the full scope of his undertaking. Puran Singh couldn't care less. Salvaging lives – which were almost lost – was what mattered most to him. Appearances and trappings – either his own or his institution's – were unimportant.

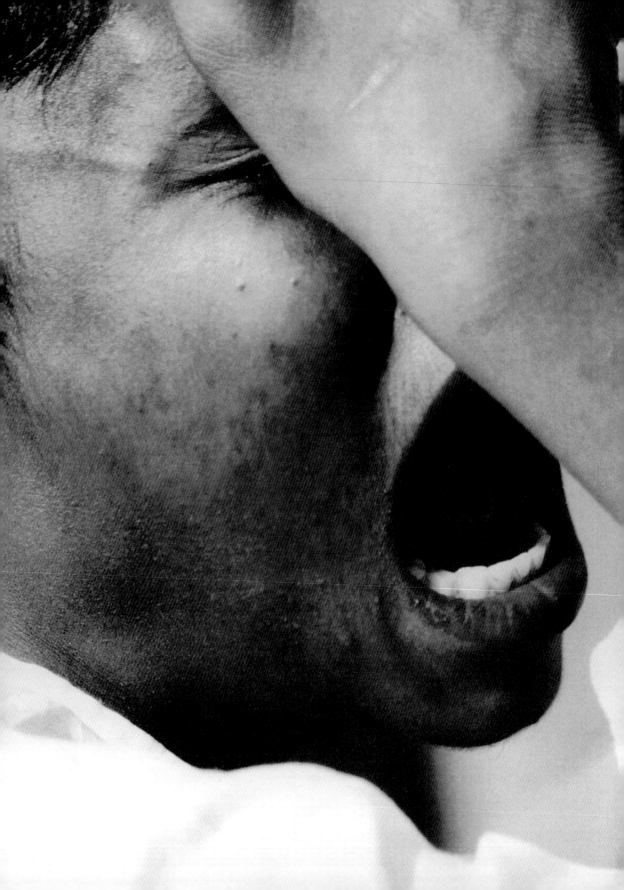

CHAPTER THREE

PINGALWARA

PINGALWARA was still a long way from realisation. Despite acquiring the property at Ram Talai, and land given by the government, there was no money to build a permanent home. Taking this too in his stride, Puran Singh turned to the *sangat* – or Sikh community – for help, since the principle of universal participation enjoins all Sikhs to set aside *daswandh* (ten per cent of their income) for charitable causes. He first called on Master Tara Singh, a prominent leader and president of the Shiromani Gurdwara Parbandhak Committee which looks after major Sikh shrines in Punjab and adjacent areas. His request to him was quite simple: would the SGPC allow him to put up sign boards outside the Golden Temple explaining Pingalwara's mission, and seeking the *sangat's* financial support?

Master Tara Singh needed no persuasion. He had seen Puran Singh's work at the Amritsar railway station, and was a long-time admirer of his singular ability to translate ideals into action. In addition to agreeing to his request, he also sanctioned an annual SGPC grant to Pingalwara which had increased to Rs. 1,50,000 per year in Puran Singh's lifetime, and has since risen to Rs. 5,50,000. The Pingalwara sign boards prepared by Puran Singh carried passages from Sikh scriptures stressing the humanitarian ethic of the faith, and its insistence on service to mankind without distinction of caste or creed. The *sangat* took the message to heart.

A fascinating aspect of Puran Singh's fledgling project

Puran Singh at the site allotted for Pingalwara and the complex as it looks today

was that even during the early years, when it needed resources desperately, supporters like the SGPC, the Punjab government and others were not allowed a say in the working of Pingalwara, because he understood intuitively that once a major organisation got its hands on Pingalwara, its ideals, aims and goals would be compromised. This was unacceptable to him. He was convinced that his own personal integrity and hands-on control were necessary to keep Pingalwara on course; to prevent the concept and its implementation from being changed beyond recognition. This was the reason for his firm stand in the fifties when the SGPC had offered to locate Pingalwara on a site within the precincts of the Golden Temple estate, in addition to a building grant of Rs. 50,000. Puran Singh had turned down the idea because, as he pointed out, "it was always possible that with the project beholden to the SGPC to this extent, any differences with the president or members in the future could seriously affect Pingalwara's working". Puran Singh was determined to keep it an institution of the Sikh *sangat*. "I want the building to be built through the collective effort of the *sangat* because Pingalwara does not function for patients of any particular religious persuasion, but for all people."

Even earlier, when the Rai Bahadur Kalyan Singh Memorial Trust had agreed to give its Ram Talai building to him, a suggestion was made that the trust's name should appear alongside Pingalwara's. Puran Singh had refused.

He next made large collection boxes of rough and ready construction with Pingalwara's name in bold letters on each, and placed them at many places in Amritsar. Ram Kishan, 70, who joined Puran Singh in 1951 and is still the *khazanchi* (treasurer) at Pingalwara, remembers the time when they used to place the first eight to ten collection boxes at busy and crowded intersections in the city, and take them away in

A makeshift caravan of cycle trailers for taking patients to the hospital >>

the evenings. No pressure was applied, no arms twisted, yet the flow of funds grew steadily as word got around of this *bhagat* (a saintly person) and his mission. Ram Kishan still has the diary in which he meticulously recorded the money collected and where and when it was spent. In the year 1952-53 (April to March), for instance, the annual income was Rs. 38,154 while the expenditure was Rs. 39,550. By 1954-55 the expenditure had shot upto Rs. 66,540. Income too increased but there was never a surplus for at least another decade.

Puran Singh recalls occasions in his writings when support for his work took different forms, and came when least expected. In early 1949, while still in the derelict house opposite the Civil Surgeon's office, he was visited one afternoon by Principal Jodh Singh who had walked all the way from Khalsa College to see him. "He was seventy years old at that time and I didn't even have a chair for him to sit on. He met each and every patient and took keen interest in the work I had started. Before leaving he gave me a donation of a hundred rupees and said I should collect five rupees a month from him as his contribution towards our work." This visit further cemented their regard for each other and they kept in close touch after the principal had moved to Patiala as vice chancellor of Punjabi University, and from there to Ludhiana after his retirement.

Mehar Singh, an engineer with the Punjab government and a regular visitor to Lahore's Dera Sahib gurdwara, was another person struck by the selflessness and confidence of this unkempt young man he saw everyday. Quite regular in setting aside one-tenth of his income (*daswandh*) for charitable causes, the impression Mehar Singh formed of Puran Singh was that beneath the deceptive personality of this tall, bony and indifferently clad youth was a core of compassion and rigorous self-discipline; of a person not easily deterred from pursuing his ideals. Convinced of his worth, he kept in touch with Puran Singh even through the trying times of partition, and when he was posted in Bathinda in the Indian part of Punjab after its truncation in 1947, he made it a point to see him whenever he visited Amritsar.

Observing Puran Singh's painstaking progress towards establishing Pingalwara, he not only donated his entire monthly *daswandh* to it but also persuaded others to help. Puran Singh records one such instance: "Mehar Singh, a tenant of Sardar Jaswant Singh Bajaj in Bathinda, brought him to Amritsar to see Pingalwara. It was an extremely difficult time for us as funds were scarce and I would go to Hall Bazar every evening for four hours with a small bell in one hand and a tin container in the other. I would keep ringing the bell to draw the attention of passersby while holding out the container for their donations. It was at such a time that Jaswant Singh came to us and on Mehar Singh's persuasion gave us Rs. 10,000 – a magnificent sum of money in those days. It helped us consolidate the foundations of Pingalwara."

Mehar Singh became a founder member and vice president of the Pingalwara Society from the time it was formed in 1957. And when construction of the main building started – for which he had helped prepare the plans – he supervised every aspect of the construction, even to the point of getting the grit for the roof washed in his presence. Settling down in Amritsar after his retirement, he used his years of experience to give Pingalwara its physical form, his involvement with it continuing till his death on 30 June 1988. "Pingalwara, as a flower blooming on the tree of Sikh culture...is all due to the cooperation and benevolence of people like Sardar Mehar Singh. Had such benefactors not come forward to buttress my cause, Pingalwara...would not

Chain Masih near the Lawrence Road entrance to Amritsar's Company Bagh and,
from left to right, Amar Nath, Abdul Hakim and Durga Das who have worked at Pingalwara for almost 50 years

exist," wrote Puran Singh of the man who had committed himself for over thirty years to Pingalwara's cause.

Another phase in their fund-raising efforts is narrated by Puran Singh's long-time associate Chain Masih who joined him in February 1952. Now 66, Masih's eyes well-up as he recalls the time when they would both stand on bitterly cold winter mornings outside Amritsar's Company Bagh where people from the exclusive residential area of Lawrence Road would come for their early morning walk. "We had no money in those days for even the basic needs of our patients, so shoes were a luxury we couldn't afford. We would stand barefoot at one of the Lawrence Road entrances to the *bagh* (garden/park), holding a rectangular piece of cloth between us, and ask the morning walkers to put their donations on it. As our feet would freeze in the cold we would stand on one foot and place the other on it to keep it warm. Then reverse the order. In this way we kept ourselves from freezing."

Chain Masih became adept at fund-raising, possibly because in addition to this experience, one of the duties assigned to him, which he still performs, was to visit regular donors all over Amritsar and collect their donations. His day begins early because he also goes before dawn to the *mandi* (wholesale market) to buy vegetables and other produce for Pingalwara's kitchen which now cooks for a thousand persons everyday.

Puran Singh obviously exercised a magnetic influence on people. In addition to Des Raj and Chain Masih, Narain Singh was another person drawn to him. As a *granthi* (custodian and reader of the Guru Granth Sahib) at Gurdwara Dera Sahib in Lahore, he had greatly admired Puran Singh's work among the needy and after Partition he too migrated to India settling down in Tarn Taran, a Sikh pilgrimage centre founded by Guru Arjan Dev, not far from Amritsar. When the two re-established contact in Amritsar, Puran Singh had nearly sixty destitutes – mostly women and children – in his care, so Narain Singh's offer to work with him was gladly accepted as another helping hand was definitely needed.

Narain Singh travelled every morning from Tarn Taran to Amritsar, returning home late in the evenings. His work entailed collecting food for Pingalwara's inmates from various well-to-do homes in the city since it has long been a tradition among old established families in north India to share food cooked in the house with those in need; sadly, this is a waning tradition now because of the new generation's indifference to it. Puran Singh admired "the diligence with which Narain Singh carried out his responsibilities", and his "genuine zeal to serve suffering people. Despite his advanced years he worked very hard and took on work which was physically demanding." He was paid one rupee and twenty five paise a day as he had a family to support. This also covered his fare from Tarn Taran and back!

There were many others who assisted Puran Singh, among them Abdul Hakim, 75, who manages the Piara Singh ward and who joined him in 1948. But Puran Singh performed the most difficult jobs himself. To use his own words: "I have swept the excreta of patients and I do so even now; I have picked up banana and other fruit-skins from the streets and do so even now; I have carried mud and bricks on my head for the upcoming buildings of Pingalwara and am ready to do so even now when I am running into my 82nd year; I have begged for the inmates from door to door and will do so even now.... I do not feel ashamed of all this."

He demanded nothing for himself on principle – which is understandable since he had no needs – but he did not hesitate to ask people to support his work. Joginder Singh, 81, whose grandfather Harnam Singh had been his mentor

Midday meals at Pingalwara: feeding time for the inmates and Puran Singh with his eating bowl

Time for play >>

The first 'buildings' at Pingalwara

in Lahore, narrates how Puran Singh would visit their home and jokingly tell his mother, Anant Kaur, that "I am an equal claimant", along with her three sons, "to our grandfather's property". When it came to Pingalwara, Puran Singh was more serious. "He felt free to walk into our house for help and I remember him asking once for a few used blankets he urgently needed for his wards." In the sixties and seventies, as Pingalwara's permanent home and its facilities grew, so did his demands which were good-naturedly described as "unending and enormous". But these, "howsoever heavy", said Puran Singh "were always met generously by the public because people are confident that behind my craze for collection is an unselfish and noble cause".

While waiting for funds to start construction on the land he had acquired for Pingalwara, Puran Singh built a few makeshift shelters on it. These were no better than shanties, but no worse than the conditions under which he was used to living. At least now they were on their own land. Even though his financial resources were already strained to the limit, Puran Singh started Pingalwara's construction in April 1961. Fortunately, an unexpected stroke of luck favoured him in the form of a generous offer by Mrs. Padmavati Duggal, widow of a distinguished Amritsar philanthropist Diwan Balkishan Duggal who had owned Amrit Talkies – one of Amritsar's oldest cinema houses. The lady offered to fund the construction of three large rooms – dedicated to the memory of her husband – in the block facing the main road. These rooms now house Pingalwara's administrative offices and a small museum which honours Puran Singh's life and work. The ground-breaking ceremony took place in April and the *ardas*, a special Sikh prayer, was offered by Bhai Kishan Singh, a former *granthi* of Gurdwara Dera Sahib in

Lahore who was aware of Puran Singh's moral fibre and intense commitment to his work. They had maintained contact after Partition, and as Kishan Singh was another link in the circle of his life Puran Singh invited him to offer invocation at this event towards which he had been working since the two first met.

A second windfall followed the first: a Rs. 15,000 grant by the Punjab Government's Central Social Welfare Board – not an inconsiderable sum of money thirty-eight years ago. Yet another handsome donation of Rs. 50,000 came by courtesy of the Amrit Parchar Sangat. These donations were important for another reason too: they provided a further impetus to the *sangat's* support which admired Puran Singh's courage in undertaking construction when he barely had money with which to feed his 150 wards. He had proved his staying power by frequently buying rations on credit and paying for them when funds arrived, which they did in increasing amounts – but only after several years of great hardship.

Though in appearance Pingalwara's buildings seemed a replication of existing hospitals, that is not how they functioned. They were built to take care of people whose congenital disabilities disqualified them for the attention which only the sick receive in hospitals. "In our country the helpless and the homeless dying on the road are a very common sight...it is taken as the inevitable fate of a human being." Puran Singh intended to redress this inhumanity at Pingalwara, his role being aptly summed up by someone who had closely observed his work: "God helps those who help themselves; Bhagat Puran Singh has vowed to help those who can't help themselves."

He found it odd that while wealthy benefactors were willing to fund major hospitals, they were unmoved by the

With overseas visitors >

The tree under which Puran Singh usually sat in Pingalwara's courtyard

<< Piara Singh Ward for communicable diseases

"spectacle of helpless persons dying on the street"; their most basic needs ignored; even their very existence overlooked. He believed India's social sector was crying out for care of the destitute and despairing, whom the hospitals refused admission. "Such an idea could only take birth in the mind of a poor and not a rich man, because the approach of each to such a social problem is radically different." Even a cursory look at India's urban landscape amply proves it, because "a rich person always thinks of endowing money and running his own independent hospital, self-contained in every respect. He thinks of providing his own doctors, his own equipment with medical and surgical apparatus...which is very costly". This is fine if there are no other hospitals around. But Puran Singh believed that where fully equipped hospitals already exist, what the common man needs "is not another...hospital, but greater boarding facilities, as he can always avail of the outdoor treatment provided by existing hospitals". He felt that wherever a hospital's outdoor facilities are inadequate, they can be expanded at far less cost than building a new hospital.

His own outlook had been shaped by his experience of many decades; by his efforts at alleviating the suffering of men, women and children no hospitals would take even though they clearly merited society's humanitarian concerns. Each experience in his life was a milestone which had brought him nearer to his goal of Pingalwara: from the time in 1925 when he had seen a gravely ill man express his gratitude on being given a bed with clean sheets ("at least here I will die in peace and comfort"); to 1934 when he had found Piara Singh abandoned by the roadside in Lahore; to his work with the refugees in Khalsa College in 1947; to the time he had tried to ease Asha Rani's last days of suffering in 1949; to that period when he had kept his wards under trees, in toilets and abandoned buildings in the forties and fifties. Each experience had helped him clarify his vision of the future.

He did not visualise Pingalwara as an institution for the sick – a perceptive view which is as valid today as it was then. He had no wish to establish a hospital. His facilities would cater to people who needed hope, and a home; who were denied human dignity by an uncaring society. Pingalwara would prove that it is possible to give specific form to social ideals. He believed there were enough good people to recognise good work. What mattered was not outward form but inner faith and strength, and the goals a person sets for himself. He knew this well. He had faced ridicule, jeers and insults because of his appearance; because of the crippled boy he had carried on his back for years; because he had not cringed at cleaning with his hands the urine, faeces, vomit and pus of people in his care; because he gave each his equal attention according to the ethics of his faith. As he put it: "Mine has been a full and meaningful life – a guru-directed journey in the service of humanity".

He believed that if he could motivate more people towards humanitarian ideals, the world would be a better place. So Pingalwara had to succeed and its philosophy to find wide acceptance since that would lead to the involvement of more people in issues of social concern – which is not the case at present. In India's villages, towns and cities the affluent stride or drive past the disabled and despairing with unseeing eyes. If they do notice them it is not with compassion or concern but with condescension and contempt; because, paradoxically, the sight of misery makes men callous. Puran Singh wanted the country's better-off segments to see and respond to the harsh, everyday Indian reality around them. Not just through the Pingalwara model, but through the print medium as well.

This brings us to the other astonishing facet of the man: his never-ending quest for knowledge and for communicating through the printed word. He writes about this aspect of his life in his reminiscences. "I do not even know how to thank the Sikh gurdwaras, their *langars*, their hospitality to travellers, the devotees who visit these gurdwaras. All these collectively became the means to my self-education.... The big libraries of Lahore provided me the opportunity to read books, journals, biographies, etc. published abroad, helped me to keep abreast of the latest developments overseas in the realm of knowledge. This exposure made me aware of important issues and also gave me a world view."

Almost entirely self-taught, he became a denizen of the libraries at Lahore and Amritsar – itself a feat of sorts considering the amount of work he put in from morning to night. That he still found time to walk considerable distances to them – with Piara always on his back – and read up on a wide variety of authors and subjects is amazing. Even more so the range of his interests: from the global arms race, oil crises and population explosion to forestry, environment, the impact of industrialization, depletion of natural resources and pollution.

He would write on these subjects far into the night. The clutter around him when he was reading, writing or taking notes had to be seen to be believed. It was enough to put any artist or writer, aspiring to an unconventional Bohemian life, to shame. He would sit – usually on the floor – surrounded by piles of newspapers, journals, books, pamphlets, clippings, crumpled balls of paper and much else, and continue unfazed through interruptions of every conceivable kind. In time he began producing an impressive body of work consisting of booklets, pamphlets, handbills and posters which were distributed free to the general public. To keep pace with his prolific output all the material was printed at Pingalwara. Starting with a single manual machine in 1956 the press now has nineteen, with about forty people working on composing, proofing, printing and distributing whatever is produced – a high percentage of which consists of reprints of Puran Singh's writings.

The two rooms of the printing press in the main Pingalwara complex are a hive of activity – the effect heightened by the dexterity with which operators work the old-fashioned manual machines installed in close proximity to each other to save space. To put Puran Singh's insistence on conservation into practice, almost half the quantity of paper used is recycled. Procured from rag pickers or government offices not only is the blank side of the paper used to print Pingalwara's material, but even the other side is over-printed in bold and bigger type faces to make for easy readability. The finished product – looking none the worse for wear – certainly works.

Explaining his emotional and cerebral involvement with this facet of his life, Puran Singh said: "I have no personal demands but my demands for Pingalwara are unending...a sizable chunk of my time is taken by my activities relating to the inculcation of social and ecological awareness among our people and that requires money, which I collect from the public."

Even amongst Indians, more versatile than most in running each other down, there has been unanimity in praise of Puran Singh's work. But since habits die hard, his writings were singled out for a particularly thick-witted comment by a well-known columnist who otherwise had high words of praise for him: "He asked me if I could persuade the Reserve

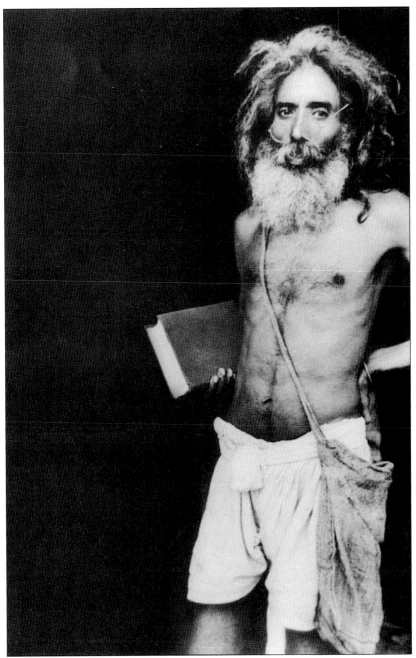

"I have no personal demands..."

Printing plant in the central complex

The main kitchen in which meals for a thousand persons are cooked everyday >>

Bank of India to grant him permission to spend a part of the donations he received from abroad for his publications. Or persuade some millionaire like Birla or Tata to finance them. This is one request of Bhagatji that I'll turn down with a clear conscience." Why? Because "as with many other good people, he has a kink in him. He must write and publish tracts which few people bother to read." Was this conclusion based on fact, and first-hand knowledge? Or because it was the smart – and snide – thing to say from a comfortable perch in Delhi for readers who expect some of their columnists to come up with at least one or two coarse comments each time?

Contrast this with Dr. Daljit Singh's view of Puran Singh: "I consider him one of the best-read persons in Amritsar who sought knowledge from every source he could, and whose own learning and writings influenced countless people. His press was very futuristic since few realised the range and effectiveness of the media in the 1950s." Daljit Singh's own formative years were spent in a household in which scholarly debates and intellectual inspiration were a daily staple since his father, Prof. Sahib Singh's work in interpreting the grammar of Guru Granth Sahib ranks as the most outstanding contribution to the study of Sikh scriptures. Interestingly, Sahib Singh was born in a Hindu household but converted to Sikhism due to his profound respect for its egalitarian principles and rational outlook.

Another quality of the man Daljit Singh points out was the extent to which he encouraged and helped aspiring scholars. Dr. Prem Singh, presently editor of *Desh Sewak*, published from Chandigarh, is one such. Educated through Puran Singh's help he did his Ph.D. in linguistics from the then USSR before teaching at Delhi University for many years. Manjit Kaur, daughter of Puran Singh's assistant Narain Singh from Tarn Taran, came to live at Pingalwara after her father's death, and with her mentor's encouragement and support qualified as a nurse. She is married, has a family, and works as a nurse at Chandigarh's prestigious Post Graduate Institute of Medical Education and Research. He also helped Manmohan Singh – younger son of Giani Achhar Singh – do his M.A., M.Ed. to become first a teacher, then headmaster of a school. The list is long. By helping the younger generation realise their aspirations, Puran Singh proved his own faith in education as the key to the future, although, ironically he himself had shunned it in his early years.

Considering Puran Singh's inability to concentrate on his studies at school, his success in communicating on so many subjects in later years is doubly impressive. This he demonstrated through his work at Pingalwara. Firstly, through the printed word; through the ample literature produced by Pingalwara's own presses. Secondly, by assigning his assistants and volunteers to distribute it extensively all over Amritsar. Wherever he himself went visiting, he too would hand out his tracts from a bag slung over his shoulder. He gained insights into subjects of critical importance by keeping himself informed of current events in India and abroad through 18 dailies to which he subscribed regularly. He also founded *Jeevan Lahar*, a magazine with a print run of 30,000 copies of which 10,000 were mailed abroad. The government closed it down after the Indian Army's assault on the Golden Temple in 1984.

The success of his communicating skills became self-evident when word of what he was doing travelled across India to many countries abroad, and was reflected in dramatic increases in Pingalwara's funding. From a hand-to-mouth existence in the early sixties, its annual budget at the time of his death in 1992 was over eleven million rupees, despite the fact that after the traumatic events of 1984, government

*Anita – whose mother is an inmate – grew up in Pingalwara;
its management arranged her marriage*

viewed overseas donations with suspicion and their flow was stopped altogether for some time. To counter this cut-off of aid Puran Singh selected two young assistants, Kirpal Singh and Harbans Singh, to mobilize support of Delhi's Sikh *sangat*. It was a wise move.

Arriving in Delhi on 21 August 1984, Kirpal Singh established regular collection points at Gurdwaras Bangla Sahib, Sis Ganj and Nanak Piao. Boxes were placed at other such centres too, and with the consent of the gurdwara authorities *sewadars* (helpers) distributed Pingalwara's literature to the *sangat*. On Sundays and special anniversaries Kirpal Singh would arrive at the gurdwaras and, with the help of assistants, pass the material to the congregations. The response was generous and annual collections from Delhi, which were around half a million rupees in 1984, rose to the figure of ten million. When normalcy returned to Punjab after some years, and with overseas Sikhs again visiting the fountainhead of their faith in Amritsar, Pingalwara's support base also expanded.

Augmentation of Pingalwara's facilities had started earlier. And not just at Amritsar. In 1975 Puran Singh purchased two plots of land in Pandori Waraich village about five kilometers from the main Pingalwara complex in Amritsar. He earmarked one of these for elderly mentally challenged patients – now numbering about fifty-five – whose ailments could benefit from the clean air and low decibel count of the rural environment. Raised in a similar environment himself, he knew this move would not only contribute to their well-being and balance but the familiar rural ambience would also be psychologically reassuring for them.

Within walking distance of this development, Puran Singh used the second plot of land to build an animal-care facility,

Bachan Singh and the tonga in which he took Puran Singh around

animals being his other great love. He had been taught by his mother to care for them at a very early age, and he always remembered her telling him that animals deserved the same love and compassion as human beings. As was to be expected, her sensitivity towards them had left a lasting impression on him. He recalled the times in his boyhood when he helped his mother draw water from the well for thirsty cattle, and "the immense pleasure and satisfaction I got on seeing the animals drink water to quench their thirst. This is when I started developing a close affinity with them".

The two tonga owners who took him around Amritsar testify to his love for animals. Hira Singh narrates an incident on an overbridge which spans the railway lines near Pingalwara. When a rather weak-looking horse of a heavily-laden tonga collapsed on the bridge, Puran Singh, who was passing by, censured its owner for his cruelty to it. The man admitted the horse was sick and said he had rested him for two days, but could not afford to any longer as he had a family to feed. When he asked him how much he earned a day and the man said Rs. 15, Puran Singh gave him Rs. 50 and told him to rest the horse for another three days. As the animal was in no condition to work even after this, Puran Singh gave the owner money to buy another horse and brought the ailing one to the safe haven of Pingalwara. Bachan Singh recalls how on the same overbridge Puran Singh would often get down and push the tonga he was travelling in to ease the strain on the horse.

He had waited many years to do something for animals who had been abused or abandoned because they were no longer useful to their owners. The time to act had come, and it took the form of a home for stray cows, buffaloes and horses at Pandori Waraich. Through proper nutritional feeds and veterinary care this extension of Pingalwara was in time

Animals instinctively sensed his love for them >>

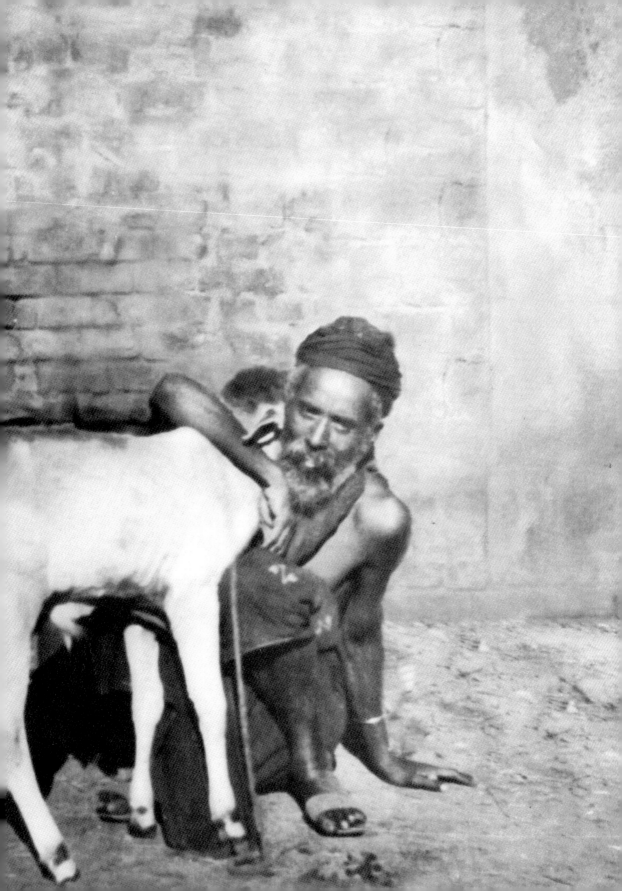

transformed into a haven for stray animals, which now number over a hundred. Interestingly, the project proved extraordinarily beneficial too since with the care lavished on them, some of the cows and buffaloes started milching again and increasing yields helped augment milk supplies for the patients and *sewadars* of Pingalwara, proving what his mother had always said, that acts of kindness carry their own rewards.

The extent of Puran Singh's concern for animals was revealed in a most unexpected manner years after his death, during a motoring trip through Punjab with his successor, Dr. Inderjit Kaur. It was a hot August day in 1999 – on the road from Amritsar to Rajewal – when Rajinder Singh, the driver of the car, suddenly stopped near a dead animal – by no means an uncommon sight on India's highways and byways which witness the daily toll vehicular traffic takes of unwary animals. More uncommon was what happened that afternoon. Rajinder Singh, an alert and energetic young man, opened the boot of the car, took out a spade, hauled the carcass of the animal some distance from the road, dug a pit, and gave it a decent burial. He then washed his hands at a nearby well before resuming the journey. The explanation offered was touching: his reflexive reaction was a result of the example set by Puran Singh in his lifetime who not only made it a point to cremate unclaimed human bodies but interred dead animals as well because, as God's creatures, they too deserve dignity in death. Whenever Puran Singh came across a carcass – even if it was highly decomposed and infested – the putrid stench did not deter him from digging a pit and burying it. On this day in August his convictions were being implemented long after his death! Rajinder Singh, who was earlier known as Rajinder Kumar before converting to Sikhism under Puran Singh's influence,

Home for stray animals at Pandori Waraich

Rajinder Singh removes a carcass and buries it in a field – animals too deserved dignity in death

was one such. He had often doubled as Puran Singh's private secretary, and was so impressed by his mentor's principles that his own commitment to them would come through in conversations with him. What is amazing is the extent to which the inspiration provided by the founder still exists in some of those who worked with him, years after his death.

In 1981 another branch of Pingalwara was opened at Goindwal, a centre of Sikh devotion on the left bank of the Beas river, about 35 kilometers from Amritsar. This historic town, surrounded by lush green fields, was founded during the pontificate of the third Sikh Guru Amar Das in the middle of the sixteenth century. Puran Singh bought a half acre of land for housing seventy-five elderly male patients, for this last extension of Pingalwara he would build in his lifetime. He wanted only men to reside at Pandori Waraich and Goindwal, while women and children would stay at Amritsar. This decision – based on practical commonsense and a sound understanding of human nature – was meant to ensure the safety of women and children who were vulnerable to abuse because of their physical and mental condition, and because of that Puran Singh wanted them under his direct supervision at Amritsar.

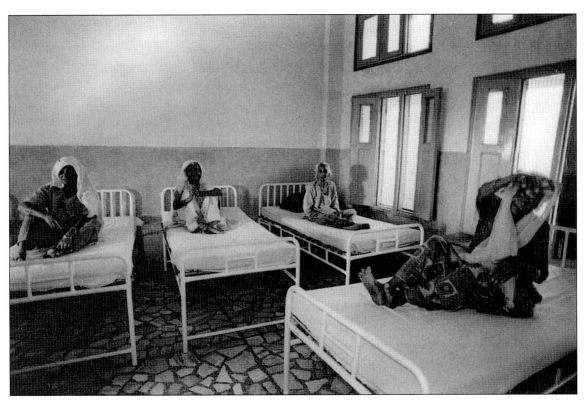

In a women's ward

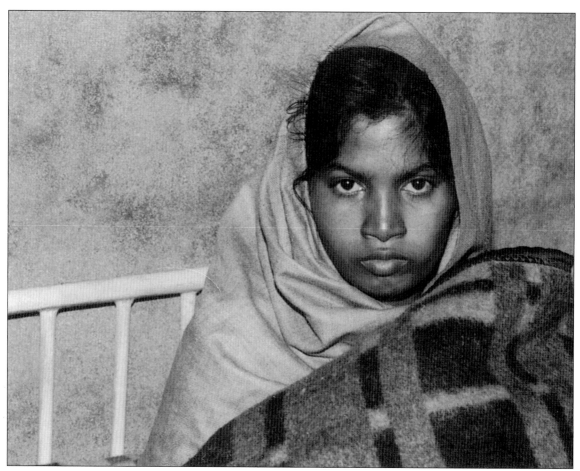

Some of Pingalwara's inmates – above and on the following pages >>>

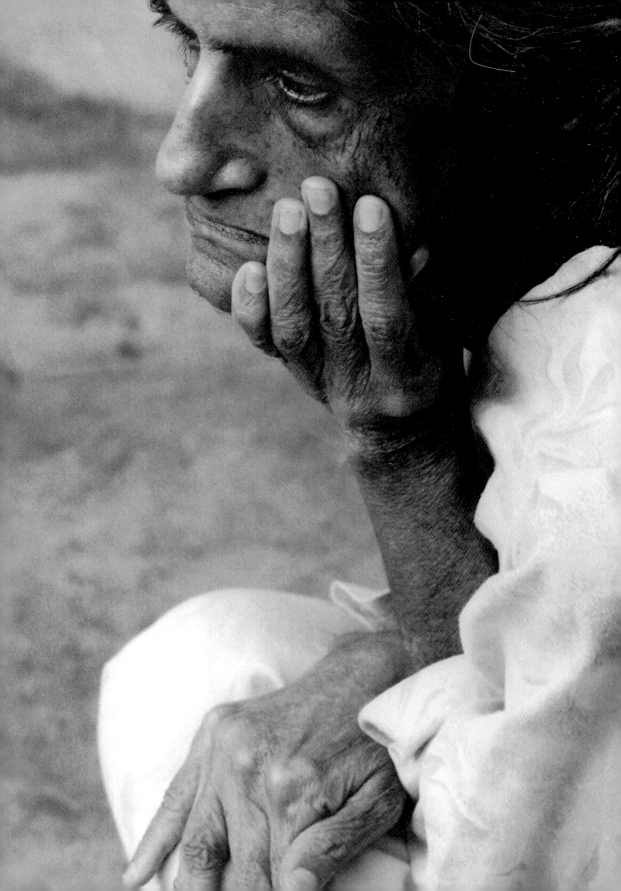

CHAPTER FOUR

THE TRANSCENDENT SPIRIT

COMMENTS on Puran Singh and his work, made over forty years ago by men like Sardar Bhagat Singh, a District and Session Judge, and Diwan Anand Kumar, Vice Chancellor of Punjab University, rarely mention his environmental concerns. They refer admiringly to this rustic, rough-hewn man's unique humanitarian mission, but ecology seldom figured in their appraisal of him. Was it because his ecological concern grew in later years? According to him he was quite "aware in 1928 that the denudation of forests in the catchment areas of hills cause floods in the plains and...I became concerned with saving forests...and creating awareness of the destructive forces which threaten our survival".

His mention of 1928 is significant as in that year a movement against felling of trees was first launched in the Kumaon and Garhwal regions of the United Provinces (later renamed Uttar Pradesh and now Uttaranchal). Villagers formed *van panchayats*, or forest committees, to resist exploitation of India's forest wealth by colonial administrators. Exploitation took many forms. One way of milking forests for richer revenues was to cut down magnificent old oak trees above altitudes of 5,000 feet, and replace them with pine forests. It was a disastrous decision for, while the broad leaves and generous spread of the majestic oaks had sheltered the earth and prevented erosion, pines provided little cover against the rains which washed the top soil of mountain slopes and carried it to the rivers below, causing silting and flooding, leading to untold destruction and misery. Another consequence of the shift from natural tree patterns to exploitative practices was loss of fodder (leaves), firewood and subsoil water which the absorbent leaf-mould of oak trees continuously replenished, but pine-needle carpets did not. All this resulted in the soil's increasing infertility due to erosion.

Resistance to the destruction of the region's centuries-old ecological balance was greatly helped by an exceptional English woman, Madelaine Slade. Drawn to India by Mahatma Gandhi's struggle she arrived on 6 November, 1925, and lived in the country for the next thirty-three years. Moving to the Garhwal hills in 1950 she soon became "painfully aware of a vital change in the species of trees which is creeping up the southern slopes, those very slopes which let down the flood waters onto the plains below...the quasi-commercial Forest Department is inclined to shut its eyes to the phenomenon because the *banj* (Himalayan oak) brings them no cash for the coffers, whereas the *chirh* pine is very profitable, yielding as it does both timber and resin".

The combative Madelaine Slade, better known by her Indian name Mira Behn, took the authorities head-on. "If the ministers who sit comfortably in New Delhi had instead to sit uneasily in the area where floods would time and again wash them out of their dwellings, the Himalayan oak would come back into its own. For there is no other remedy." She was unimpressed by the excuses offered by forest officials. "They tell one the oak cannot grow on such steep slopes as *chirh* pines, whereas I have seen oaks growing on almost perpendicular mountain slopes, and owing to their stronger and deeper roots they hold the mountainside better than the *chirh* pines. They will tell one that the *chirh* pine needles can be turned into good manure for the fields, whereas any

Mahatma Gandhi with Mira Behn (Madelaine Slade) in Switzerland, 1931

compost mixed with these needles ruins the soil. I have made such compost myself and learnt this fact to my cost...the *chirh* pine is the easiest thing in the world to propagate, it sows itself and grows like a weed...naturally the staff [of the Forest Department] likes such an easy and profitable crop."

Puran Singh, seemingly unlettered, had kept himself informed of these distant developments and writing admiringly of Mira Behn had handsomely acknowledged his indebtedness to her: "I took to heart the warnings of Mira Behn expressed in her articles on the havoc caused by floods, and did my best to distribute leaflets and pamphlets on a mass scale to the people to create an awakening about this ecological crisis...."

Yet another English disciple of Gandhi, Catherine Mary Heilemann, more popularly known as Sarla Behn, provided equally vigorous support to conservation of the Garhwal region in the 1940s by exhorting villagers to rise against the systematic destruction of their forest wealth.

The next major turn in the unfolding drama came in the early seventies when Chandi Prasad Bhatt and Sunderlal Bahuguna spearheaded the latest phase in the struggle to save the endangered forests from a combination of rapacious entrepreneurs and callous authorities. Their work gave a further boost to Puran Singh's interest in ecology. Bahuguna became involved at the urging of the Gandhian, Acharya Vinoba Bhave, who asked him to take the message of *gram swaraj* (self-sufficient village republics) to the Himalayan villages in 1960. Leading a group of Sarvodaya activists Bahuguna walked from village to village from the border of Nepal to that of Himachal Pradesh, and what he saw distressed him greatly. "It was in 1963 that I reported in an article published in *Hindustan* [a Hindi daily published in New Delhi], that there was a new danger to the country from

Top: Sarla Behn (Catherine Heilemann). Bottom: Sunderal Bahuguna

the Himalayas – the danger of floods. I had seen bald hills all around. But nobody listened to this warning because to most people floods simply meant more embankments...."

What he had predicted came true. A massive cloudburst over the Kuari Khal mountains in the Garhwal Himalayas during the night of 20 July, 1970 caused the worst-ever floods in the Tehri-Garhwal region, with the swollen Alaknanda River wreaking havoc along its banks. This tragedy gave birth to the Chipko movement. Started by people of Mandal village in Chamoli district, the strategy behind Chipko (it literally means 'embrace'), was stunningly simple and effective: each villager hugged an *ash* tree to prevent its felling by a sports goods factory. Often villagers had themselves bound to trees. As word of this novel form of resistance to injustice spread, it not only stirred the imagination of that region's people, but also of people in the plains and cities. And "when the sports goods company was allotted *ash* trees in the adjacent Kedarnath Valley, the village communities there acted as the Mandal villagers had done". In March 1974, following a big agitation at Reni near Joshimath, "village women, led by Gaura Devi [of the local Mahila Mangal Dal], drove the axemen out of the forest".

The Chipko movement had come to stay. And when Bahuguna, one of its two principal founders – the other being Chandi Prasad Bhatt – visited Mira Behn in Austria in 1981, he gratefully acknowledged her role as one of the movement's chief inspirations. "She was overjoyed when she heard" of its success. Bahuguna, was himself influenced by his wife Vimala Nautial, who before her marriage was a disciple and co-worker of Sarla Behn. By a sad coincidence, Sarla Behn (Catherine Mary Heilemann) died eleven days before Mira Behn's death in July 1982.

What is remarkable when seen in retrospect is how the

lives and goals of these strong, socially aware and committed people overlapped, and the extent to which they inspired each other. Although Puran Singh never met any of them, the logic of their arguments left a deep impression on him, compelling him to embrace the cause of ecology as enthusiastically as he had of society's uncared segments. Since alleviating human misery – in whatever form – was his life's mission, his interest in the physical environment made perfect sense, as a degraded environment added to human misery. By failing to understand this, people get an incomplete picture of him. His increasing preoccupation with ecology shows a mind working at many levels, constantly posing questions, searching for answers, looking at society's problems, broadening his own understanding of national concerns, to which end three readers kept him informed of what was published in newspapers, magazines and books. They also kept countless clippings for him. This explains why Puran Singh published as extensively as he did, including a collection of essays, articles and press reports, some of which – published over thirty years ago – were reproduced in a book, *Peril of Survival*. Several carry introductory notes by him, pledging his "preparedness to immediately yoke myself tirelessly and unceasingly to the effort to create a deeper awareness...of the destructive forces which threaten our survival".

An unsettling article, written by Partap Singh, chief conservator of forests, Punjab, and published in *The Tribune* of 1 July, 1957, especially disconcerted him. After tracing the destruction of "great and ancient civilizations from the valleys of the Nile and Euphrates, to those of Syria and Greece", to India's "own Indus basin as revealed by the ruins of Mohenjodaro and Harappa", the writer came to the conclusion that: "These civilizations were destroyed not so much by foreign hordes as by the senseless destruction of trees mostly by the people themselves. Deprived of the protection once afforded by trees, homes, lands and aqueducts became choked and buried by sands" washed down by floods or the prevailing winds.

"The bitter lesson which must be learnt," warned the forest official, is that "no work of man, whether a town, factory, field, an orchard, road, canal, mine or dam, can survive without the benevolent protection of trees. Trees alone can protect material civilization, and its advance is therefore determined by the degree to which trees in a country have been preserved." What concerned Puran Singh most was the immediacy of the threat to his beloved Punjab. "In our own Punjab state," wrote Partap Singh, "trees are being mercilessly cut under one pretext or another, either to meet the demands of fuel or because they are impediments to other forms of land use such as agriculture, with the result that lands are progressively becoming more dessicated, producing lesser yields per acre." To illustrate this, he pointed out that during the digging of the Bhakra Canal "the profiles of soils exposed showed that even in the southern districts like Hissar and Ferozepur, the lower horizons are sandy loam, even a clayey loam, whereas the top six inches to a foot has become more sandy and thereby lost much of its fertility". Even more telling was that "live sand dunes can be seen between Jullundur City and Jullundur Cantonement...[with] mounds of sand rising rapidly on either side of the roads".

In a ten-point memorandum of his personal beliefs – which carries Puran Singh's signature – six relate to conservation of the environment; of these, three concern trees. Which is not altogether surprising. "Planting of trees," he once observed "is described in India's ancient texts as an act of great kindness." His mother too had instilled a love of trees in him. And he recalls how she made him nurture them. "My mother had planted three trees by the side of the village pond which my father had got built. The trees were around 76 years old (in 1988) and they are still standing, keeping my mother's memory alive. I remember from about the age of eight, my mother would take me with her when she went to visit the trees, and she would make me water them." Her influence on him had lasted his entire lifetime. On a wall of the Pingalwara complex this warning is written in large letters, "the green forest cover in India is being reduced at the rate of ten lakh (one million) and fifty thousand hectares every year. If this process of hewing the jungle continues, India would turn into a vast desert...."

Apart from the three points in his memorandum on the importance of planting and caring of trees, the remaining seven emphasise the need to control the growth of population; eat simple food and wear simple clothes; help reduce unemployment by wearing hand-spun cloth; lead austere lives; take note of how water and land are crying out for attention; protect God's gift of nature; use as little diesel and petrol as possible.

He fuelled his campaign to create ecological awareness with a crusader's zeal, incessantly warning people about the destruction of the natural environment. His own early years were spent breathing clean air, eating corn, wheat and vegetables uncontaminated by chemical fertilizers, drinking pure water and wholesome milk, inhaling air free of poisonous fumes, and walking eight to ten miles a day. He had lived in cities as well, seen the relentless onslaught of technology and its uncritical acceptance by government and citizens alike. With the Pingalwara complex located across the road from Amritsar's busy bus terminus, he had seen the

Puran Singh – with Piara on a trailer – on his way to the Darbar Sahib >>

ਜੀ ਗੁਰੂ ਕੀ
ਗਰੀ ਦੀ
ਬਾ ਵਧਾਉਣ
ਵਾਲੀ ਸੰਸਥ
ਪਿੰਗਲਵਾੜੇ
ਚ ਫੇਰੀ
ਪਾ ਕੇ ਜਾਣ
ਜੀ।

ਸਾਹਿਬ ਦੇ
ਵਿਚ ਸਾੜੇ ਜਾਣ ਵਾਲੇ (ਇਨ ਸੌ ਤੋ ਵੱਧ)

126	ਹੱਡੀਆਂ ਦੇ ਪਲਸਤਰ ਵਾਲੇ	
52	ਅਪਰੰਗ ਵਾਲੇ	
37	ਦੁੱਧ ਤੇ ਪਲਣ ਵਾਲੇ	
4	ਪੜ੍ਹ ਜਾਣ ਵਾਲੀਆ ਕੁੜੀਆਂ	
52		

ਇਸ ਗੱਡੀ ਵਿਚ ਬਰਾਤ
ਰਨ ਸਿੰਘ ਲੂਲੇ ਪਿਆਰ
ਸਿੰਘ ਨੂੰ ਸੀ ਦਰਬਾਰ

air fouled by hydrocarbons, nitrogen oxide and such. Through his experience of human afflictions and reading far into the night, he understood the danger carbon monoxide and such gases posed, and the permanent disablement they could cause: from cardiovascular complications and cancer, to kidney, liver, respiratory and other disorders.

Conscious of the deadly fallout of diesel and petrol fumes in the atmosphere, he preferred to walk or take a tonga (horse-drawn carriage), or bicycle. Since the only way he knew of persuading people was by personal example, he seldom travelled by car or bus, and one of the questions he invariably asked people was – how many miles had they walked that day. He recommended eight to ten miles. During 1948, when he had settled his wards in Amritsar's railway station compound, he would place the ailing persons on a handcart and push it all the way to the Guru Tegh Bahadur Hospital to get them treated. Dr. Madanjit Kaur, of Amritsar's Guru Nanak Dev University says, "he would insist you should come to visit him either on a tonga, or on foot". His long-time confidant, SS Rahi, Pingalwara's general manager, corroborates this. "If you respect me," Puran Singh would tell people "come to me walking. Tell your driver to pick you up later." As for himelf, he scrupulously avoided cars and was extremely uncomfortable when in his eighties he had to travel in one to Delhi, at the invitation of the then President of India, Giani Zail Singh. His objection to cars was revolutionary at a time when the world had yet to start debating problems of pollution which are now causing global concern. During the early years, he would take his patients to various hospitals, from the different locations he had been in, by pushcart. One long-time observer of those years recalled the times he would transport his mental patients on a handcart. "Sometimes he would be stranded at the railway crossing for over an hour when trains were being shunted about. He never complained even if he had to wait in the scorching heat, or rain, or on cold winter days." Since he had no helpers, this period of great hardship strengthened him both physically and in his beliefs.

To reinforce his advocacy of walking, Puran Singh reminded people that "all great teachers were walkers – Buddha, Shankaracharya, Guru Nanak, Vivekananda, Gandhi, Vinoba Bhave". But walking was only one of the ways in which he emulated them. Just as some of the Indian savants opposed conventional wisdom and developed their own philosophical formulations, Puran Singh too was radically different in his thinking. If Vinoba Bhave, traversed India on foot to persuade wealthy landowners to donate some of their land to the landless, Puran Singh compelled people to recognise the degrading conditions of their less fortunate fellow-humans and urged them to generously support efforts to make their lives more meaningful.

The bicycle became his preferred means of transporting the handicapped. Placing them on a cycle-trailer, then hitching it to his bicycle, he would be on his way whilst others were still debating what to do. For long-distance travel he preferred trains because they carried more people and used relatively less energy than cars, buses and trucks.

Interestingly, towards the end of the 1990s, use of the cycle for personal and cargo transportation which Puran Singh had put to good use decades earlier, was being taken very seriously by New York's Institute for Transportation and Development Policy as a 'human-powered vehicle for the millennium'. Its Executive Director Dr. Walter Hook recently regretted the tendency of India's civic leaders to get rid of rickshaws, especially since the new ones with six-speed gears, lights and caliper brakes, and such are destined to become vehicles of the future, adding that they were already operating in over 40 US cities.

His inclusion of the larger human habitat in the ambit of his concerns was also an act of vision, not eccentricity, according to Dr. Inderjit Kaur, his successor. She views him as "a pathfinder who warned ordinary men and women of the dangers inherent in the reckless pursuit of technology for its own sake, as it would devastate all the treasures of this earth...." She is clear that in the final analysis his inspiration came from the spiritual sources of his beliefs. "Bhagatji regarded the earth as a holy shrine of the Lord, after Guru Nanak's concept.... Within the Universe, Earth was created as a Shrine, and polluting its atmosphere was an act of sacrilege." A line in the daily prayers of the Sikhs sums it up: *"Pawan guru pani pita mata dharat mahat...."* which means "air is the guru, water is the father, and earth is the great mother of all...." In urging people to respect the environment Puran Singh was reemphasising what the Sikh scriptures have always stressed.

He was immensely appreciative of the fact that Sunderlal Bahuguna, the man he had always admired but never met, was campaigning on another crucial front as well: the conservation of water and air. The country's notorious indifference towards their conservation had set it on a dangerous course, and as Bahaguna was rightly pointing out "pure water and clean air being the by-products of forests...with the senseless hacking of trees in the catchment areas, water would become scarce, and access to fresh water would be a serious problem in the future". He suggested a three-A-formula for water conservation: "austere use of water; alternatives to minimise wastage; afforestation on an extensive scale to retain a perfectly balanced hydrological system".

Dr. Inderjit Kaur with SS Rahi

Puran Singh, as was his custom, ordered a large number of reprints of an article which carried Bahuguna's warning and distributed it extensively to warn people of the danger of water shortages in the coming years. What is amusing – and rather quaint at the same time – is the manner in which he reproduced articles and book excerpts with supreme indifference to copyright matters and such. He knew what he was doing was right because he was doing it for humanity at large and not for himself. And that was good enough for him!

During the hours he spent avidly reading the many crises facing India, what disturbed him greatly were reports of the rapidly increasing population which the country was ill-equipped to handle. Neither the cities, hospitals, schools, colleges or universities nor the nation's potential for providing employment to its exploding population were capable of meeting the challenge. He had seen the figures double between 1947 to the start of the 1980s when the number had risen to around 700 million. He had also seen the social tensions generated by the increasing affluence of new industrial-technological elites, and the decreasing living standards of the masses over 40 per cent of whom lived below the poverty line. The ill effects of some of their development policies on India's social fabric were being ignored by the planners, so the foremost national priority, it seemed to him, should be to curb the country's runaway population.

He was fond of quoting an article which had placed things in their correct perspective. "Poverty in India will grow if the emphasis continues to be on industralisation – because industry is not able to provide even half a million jobs a year while more than seven million enter the job market every year. Six times as many people are employed on the land as in government, industry and trade put together. At present the unemployed and underemployed number 80 million. If jobs are not created faster there will [soon] be 200 million unemployed...."

His own approach was down-to-earth, and no less pertinent. "When God created man and woman he did not guarantee that each one born would be fed, clothed and housed, irrespective of whether he lived his life intelligently or otherwise. The history of countless famines throughout the world show how people in hundreds of thousands died due to them. In India too, over the last 100 years, around 30 famines took a heavy toll of human beings, farm oxen and milching cows. They died in lakhs, like ants. Others were uprooted from their homes and went trekking hundreds of miles away in search of food and water and new locations to live their lives in." After elaborating further, Puran Singh would come to the central theme of his message. "There is nothing wrong with marriage. But in the context of marriage it is necessary for each person to understand that his or her role is not merely to get married and produce children, but also to think how they will meet their childrens' future needs for food, clothing, education and much else." He was not in favour of going into life blindfolded, and was fond of recalling the ancient Indian tradition by which people remained celibate for many reasons, one of them being their reluctance to add to the numbers of unwanted children whose lives were wasted away because of their parents', and an uncaring society's, indifference towards them.

In the twilight of his life, at the age of seventy-five, public recognition of Puran Singh's steadfast commitment to his humanitarian mission seemed to be finally coming, with the Union Government's Ministry of Social Welfare recommending his name for the Padma Vibhushan, India's second highest civilian award. After the then Minister, Dr. PC Chunder, fully endorsed his ministry's recommendation, it was assumed the Home Ministry would also agree. But it did not. Chunder was no less baffled than his officials when in 1979 Puran Singh was instead awarded the Padma Shri: the lowest in the rung of civilian awards, and not the second highest they had recommended! Even though it mattered little to the recipient, who was not even aware of the move to honour him, it is still puzzling why the importance of his spectacular achievement was scaled down? Were there other criteria he didn't meet?

Interestingly, Mother Teresa was given the same award in September 1962, when the Missionaries of Charity had been in existence for just twelve years. When Puran Singh received the Padma Shri, he was seventy-five and his personal mission had begun over fifty years earlier. There is yet another postscript to the above: just days after Mother Teresa received the Nobel Prize in Oslo in 1979, the Indian government decided to bestow the nation's highest honour, the Bharat Ratna, on her. At the award-giving ceremony President Sanjiva Reddy rightly observed: "She embodies in herself compassion and love of humanity as few in history have done.... Her entire life has been a personification of service and compassion. These are the imperatives of human existence which are generally affirmed in words but denied in actions." But were Puran Singh's compassion and love of humanity any less?

If the government could not rise above its strange reluctance to acknowledge the value and spirit of volunteerism – which alone can encourage people into taking on some of society's social burdens – others were more generous. In 1990 he received the Harmony Award from the Organisation of Understanding and Fraternity, and in 1991 the then Prime Minister, Chandra Shekhar, presented him the Lok Rattan

Award. The same year Punjab's Human Rights Society conferred the Bhai Kanhaiya Award on him. As a government official aptly pointed out, the underlying irony lay in the fact that the recipient considered all this an unnecessary intrusion on his time. Puran Singh even returned the Padma Shri award after the Indian Army's assault on the Golden Temple in June 1984. His conscience wouldn't allow him to keep an honour bestowed by a government which had shown no compunction in mounting an attack on this hallowed symbol of the Sikh faith – particularly as he had always held that a person like him "who had literally built Pingalwara from the sidewalks upwards, could never have achieved as much without the strength and support I received from my implicit and abiding faith in Sri Darbar Sahib...."

But those who had watched his mission with growing admiration over the years were determined to ensure international recognition for his extraordinary dedication. And so a move to get him the Nobel Prize was initiated in 1992 by the Guru Gobind Singh Foundation based in Washington, DC. Recommending his name to the Nobel Committee, Dan Burton, Member of the US House of Representatives, wrote: "Given Bhagat Puran Singh's outstanding devotion and service to India's less fortunate, I believe he is truly deserving of the Nobel Peace Prize. In my opinion, he exemplifies both the spirit and objectives of this prestigious honor." Paul Martin, MP in the House of Commons, Ottawa, Canada, also wrote to the Committee. "We respectfully submit that at times of hardships and global reduction of volunteer involvement, your organisation would have a tremendous opportunity to send a clear message to the world by choosing Mr. Puran Singh." But sadly, he died on 5 August 1992 – at the very time efforts were being made to get his singular achievements known around the world.

Not that he was entirely unknown at the time of his death at the age of 88. People in India and abroad were already drawn to this amazing man by the selflessness with which he had dedicated his entire life to his work. Many had been to Pingalwara on their visits to the Golden Temple, and returned in disbelief – often in awe – at what they saw there: an unassuming, weather-beaten votary of the poor, indifferently dressed in handspun clothes, sitting under a tree in the courtyard of the Pingalwara complex with reams of paper around him. Or ministering to the needs of the inmates. Or eating a spartan meal from a metal bowl. Or sleeping at night on the floor of one of the wards whilst the patients slept on the beds around him. The experience of seeing this man in the setting he had created with grit and determination left few unmoved. And many members of the Sikh diaspora, when they returned to the countries they now lived in, set up centres to raise funds for Pingalwara.

One amongst the many overseas Sikhs who played a leading role in motivating her compatriots was Bibi Avinash Kaur Kang of Ontario, Canada. She not only established a charitable society there for aiding Pingalwara, but now has a website as well dedicated to help the cause. She recalls that after her first meeting with Puran Singh in 1987 he had told her "*Bibi, waapis ja ke Pingalwara da dhyan rakhin*" (Bibi, when you go back, keep Pingalwara in mind); which she certainly did. Starting with her first cheque for Rs.1100 in 1987, she was collecting around C$ 1,80,000 a year by 1998-99. Other enthusiastic supporters of Pingalwara, like Sardar Gurbaksh Singh Sibia and Bibi Chanan Kaur of the UK, Bibi Jitinder Kaur of the USA and Sardar Raman Singh of Dubai have also kept Pingalwara's flame alive as have others in India and abroad whose support is a reaffirmation of the Sikh spirit of *sewa*.

August 5, 1992

The personal 'possessions' he left behind

< End of an epoch

One of the many moving tributes on Puran Singh's death was paid by Amrik Singh Bhatia who at the age of 10 had first seen Puran Singh alight from the truck which had brought him from Pakistan to Amritsar on 18 August, 1947. Said Bhatia, "The ominous moment came to pass on Wednesday, 5 August, 1992, when at 2.30 p.m. the mightiest heart of our times which had warmed so many with hope and affection, ceased beating once and for all."

The quintessential Puran Singh with a dying inmate >

CHAPTER FIVE

PURAN SINGH IN HIS OWN WORDS

PINGALWARA – ITS PHILOSOPHY AND PURPOSE

EVERY sick person who is physically unfit to earn his livelihood has the right to be looked after by philanthropists and organisations working in the field of social service and charity. This must be seen as the basic and fundamental right of every human being.... Pingalwara came into existence with the avowed purpose of saving persons with different afflictions from dying unattended on the sidewalks of the cities.... It is a heartless society which does nothing for those destitute and unattached mental patients who can be saved if their problems are addressed in time. My work is not confined to any religion or country, it is universal for all living beings. I have worked throughout my life under the patronage of Sikh Gurdwaras without which I could have achieved nothing.

Thoughts and Writings of Bhagat Puran Singhji,
A Pingalwara Publication, Amritsar, 2000, pp. 58-60.

FAITH IN GOD

I believe that God is always present around me. I am constantly aware of this fact. That is why I never hesitate to take on any kind of work. In 1947, even before the Principal of

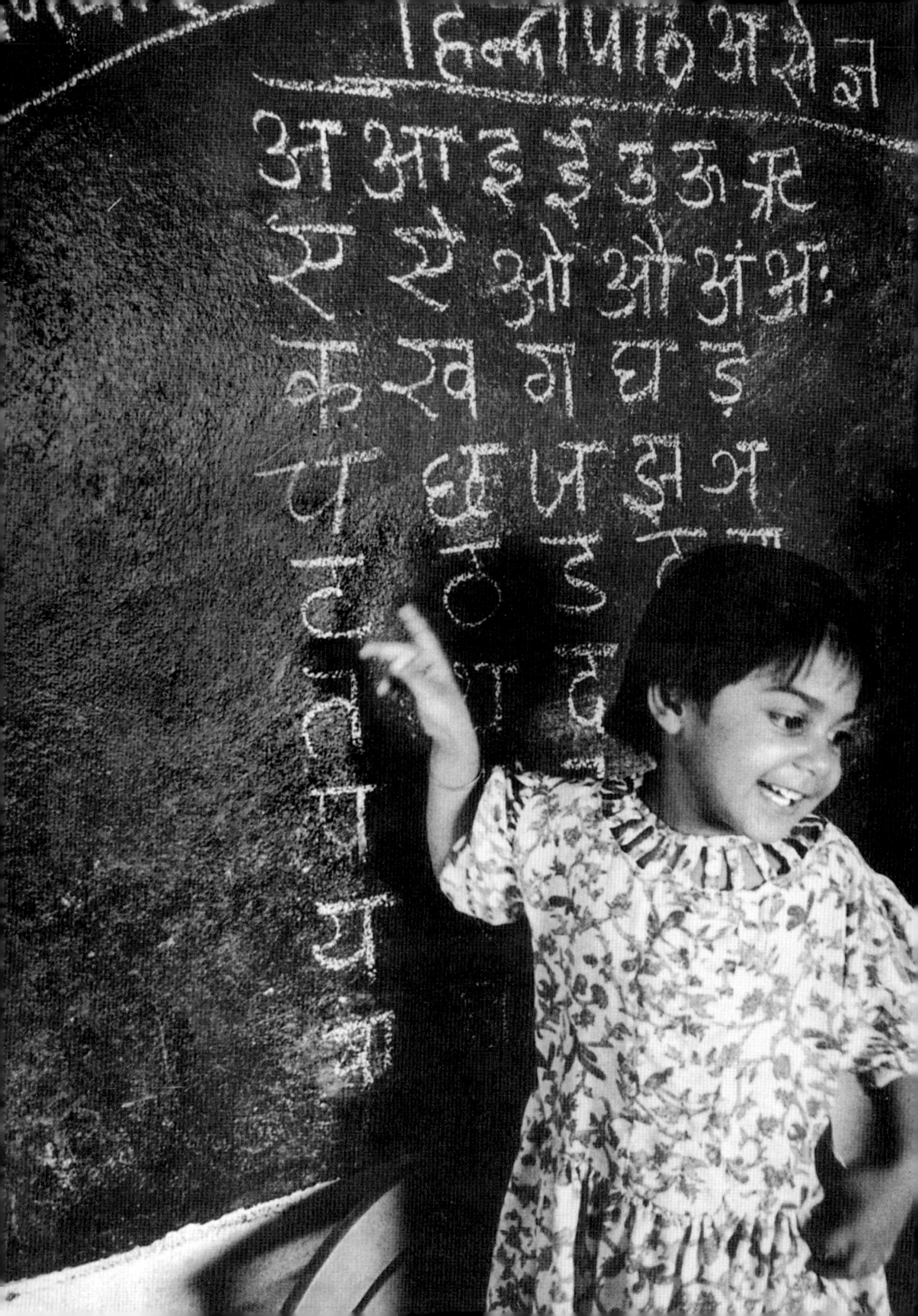
अ आ इ ई उ ऊ ऋ
ए ऐ ओ औ अं अः
क ख ग घ ङ
च छ ज झ ञ

Amritsar's Khalsa College could ask me to look after the crippled and infirm refugees on the campus, I volunteered to take care of them. This was not easy work as those in my care were suffering from dysentery and typhoid, in addition to those who were physically handicapped. They were covered with their own faeces and it was extremely difficult to keep them clean. Because of my faith in God, I was able to perform this voluntary service even before being formally asked by the [college] principal. I continued to work with my hands even after the refugee camp was wound up on 1 December, 1947. This social work is of great significance and I consider it my moral duty to write about it.... I did not have the backing or support of any rich individual or organization. But I never despair and have always remained cheerful and optimistic.

Kahaniyan,
A Pingalwara Publication, 2nd ed., Amritsar, 1996, p. 13.

A financially poor person like me established the institution of Pingalwara literally from the sidewalks and achieved so much single-handedly only because of:
– My implicit faith in the Darbar Sahib, Amritsar.
– The *sangat* of Gurdwara Dera Sahib, Lahore, which was the first to watch my work and extend its support to me.
– The *sewadars* of Dera Sahib who helped me greatly.

Be-ghar Jawan Istri,
A Pingalwara Publication, Amritsar, 1999.

I am reminded of my own transformation at Gurdwara Dera Sahib of Sri Guru Arjan Dev ji, Lahore. The programme I had set before myself by beginning my life of humanitarianism and patriotism under the patronage of that shrine has now found its fulfilment in the shape of multifarious

< Manjot, who was abandoned as an infant by her father

humane and educational activities of Pingalwara which I am
serving now.

Why Men Must Work
A Pingalwara Publication, Amritsar, 1997, p. 4.

MY MOTHER'S INFLUENCE

It is a constant source of pride for me that my mother who
was unlettered, instilled the right values in me. She had only
heard of the ancient sages and their religious philosophy.
She told me fascinating stories of their ideology and motivated me greatly in my life. I owe my desire to serve all living beings to her. She prepared me for the revolutionary path
I chose in life.

Kahaniyan, p. 31.

My mother gave me more love than any mother can give
her son. She underwent great hardships for me – the maxi-
mum any mother can for her son. She sacrificed a lot to bring
me up and educate me.... Once she came to meet me at
Khanna. In order to save some money she did not purchase
the train ticket from a station near Khanna, where she had
disembarked from the Montgomery train. She tried to board
the train after it had started moving and fell down. She was
injured on her head and would have surely died had the
train been moving faster.

Kahaniyan, pp. 83-84.

Once, in our village, someone gave my mother four *puris*
and *karah parshad*. She walked eight kilometers to my school
at Khanna to bring these to me because it gave her great satisfaction to watch me eat. Such was her devotion to me.

Kahaniyan, p. 84.

<< Darbar Sahib

My mother would go to any lengths and face any obstacles to finance my education.... My father was least concerned – he went through no hardships nor made sacrifices to educate me. His love for me was not as deep as my mother's. Had my mother died, my father would not have worked so hard – as my mother did – to pay for my schooling. My mother slaved for me because she had my welfare at heart. She blessed me with these words of Guru Arjan Dev from Guru Granth Sahib:

> *Even if for a moment you forget to take God's name*
> *His name should always be ingrained in your heart*
> *And you should remember to take it*
> *With every breath of your body.*

Kahaniyan, pp. 229-30.

Personal Service or *Sewa*

I carried on with my life's mission from the Khalsa College, the Chief Khalsa Diwan, the sidewalk opposite the railway station and under a *bodh* tree in front of the Guru Tegh Bahadur Hospital for one and a half years. Despite being poor, my trust in God provided the inspiration for this work. It was this faith which gave me the resoluteness to personally go to peoples' houses and ask for food for my wards. I would visit houses in Model Town everyday, the eating places opposite the railway station, and the railway staff quarters to collect food. I had no assistant in those days. I looked after every need of my patients single handedly – picking up their excreta, cleaning them, giving them their medicines, feeding and washing their utensils, putting them on a handcart and pushing them all the way to the hospital.

Kahaniyan, pp. 34-35.

Puran Singh with Piara – his "biggest source of strength"

PIARA – MY INSPIRATION

The cripple Piara has been the biggest source of strength in my life. Had I not found him, I would not have achieved anything in life – nor established Pingalwara which has earned me recognition and respect. For eighty years I have led a disciplined life inspired by the innocence and trust of Piara. God mercifully gave me the physical strength to single-handedly look after crippled and homeless destitutes, with no financial resources, to fall back upon and with Amritsar's streets as our hearth and home.

Kahaniyan, p. 26.

In 1936 Piara fell seriously ill and his high fever did not come down for a very long time. I spent almost seven months in a hospital in Lahore during his treatment there and even tried the Ayurvedic Hospital to cure him. I prayed to God and told Him: I have never asked you for anything in my life nor ever will again if you spare Piara's life, because he is what I treasure most. Please do not take him away from me. My life would be empty without him.

Kahaniyan, p. 239.

Today, on 2 June, 1992, I am completing my 88th year. Piara is alive and he is around 62 years of age.... A short while after I had found Piara, a doctor had told me that cripples like him do not live beyond 30 years.... Today doctors are amazed by the fact that Piara is the first cripple who is over sixty years old and is still alive.

Chaunviyan Shaksiyatan,
A Pingalwara Publication, Amritsar, 1998, p. 103.

I never got married. Consequently, I was not going to get

any sons or grandsons. For this reason God gave me Piara, who would always remain a child. His child-like pranks are very amusing and if anyone is sad, they just have to watch Piara and his antics for a while to forget their problems and start smiling. I am the most fortunate person in this world to have got Piara, whom I consider to be a blessing from God.... Piara was like a garland around my neck. He would never agree to stay away from me even for a minute, nor could I leave him alone since he is physically handicapped, his legs and hands are lifeless, and he cannot speak. He needs constant care as he cannot even sit up by himself without support. During the early days, I always had Piara on my back while tending to my other patients.

Chaunviyan Shaksiyatan, p. 104 and *Kahaniyan*, pp. 12-13.

CHILDREN

Mankind gives pride of place to children and their upkeep. For this reason orphanages have been set up all over the world to look after orphaned children. Unfortunately people in India are not aware that orphanages in the country refuse to admit or give shelter to deformed children who cannot look after themselves. Handicapped children have nowhere to go.

Adarshak Jeewan Layee Sedhan,
A Pingalwara Publication, Amritsar, 1999, p. 4.

POLLUTION AND THE ENVIRONMENT

Everything that concerns all living creatures is of interest to me.... The pollution of the atmosphere with carbon dioxide and other gases can be checked if trees are grown on a large scale. This is the only way of checking accumulation of poisonous gases. Thus, the future of the human race depends upon the planting of trees.

Thoughts and Writings of Bhagat Puran Singhji, p. 60.

I have kept an eye on the writings of environmentalists appearing in newspapers and journals and transmitting their messages full of warnings [about impending disasters] which could manifest themselves in the shape of floods, desertification and droughts. My publicity campaign commenced in the beginning of the 1950s.... In 1952 India's forest officials decided to raise the forest cover of the country from 21 per cent to 33 per cent, but the area has been diminishing unabated and unchecked since then as a result of the indiscriminate depletion and denudation of forests, until now, in 1988, it is reduced to only 11 per cent. My publicity campaign was [intended] to be an early warning of the long-term need for afforestation in the country.... There is a serious problem of ecological imbalance, putting the very survival of man at stake. The sooner man becomes aware of this problem and solves it, the better.

Plant or Perish,
A Pingalwara Publication, Amritsar, 1999, pp. 4-5.

ECONOMY

From *Young India* I learnt that British colonial rulers ruined the traditional village economy of rural India, where more than 80 per cent of its people live, by imposing their exploitative economic policies over us. I also read a lot about the impact of the industrial revolution and how machine-made goods found their way to every corner of India.... In face of this competition, cottage industries in rural areas faced ruin, causing great economic hardships to people. They

Two inmates of Pingalwara >>

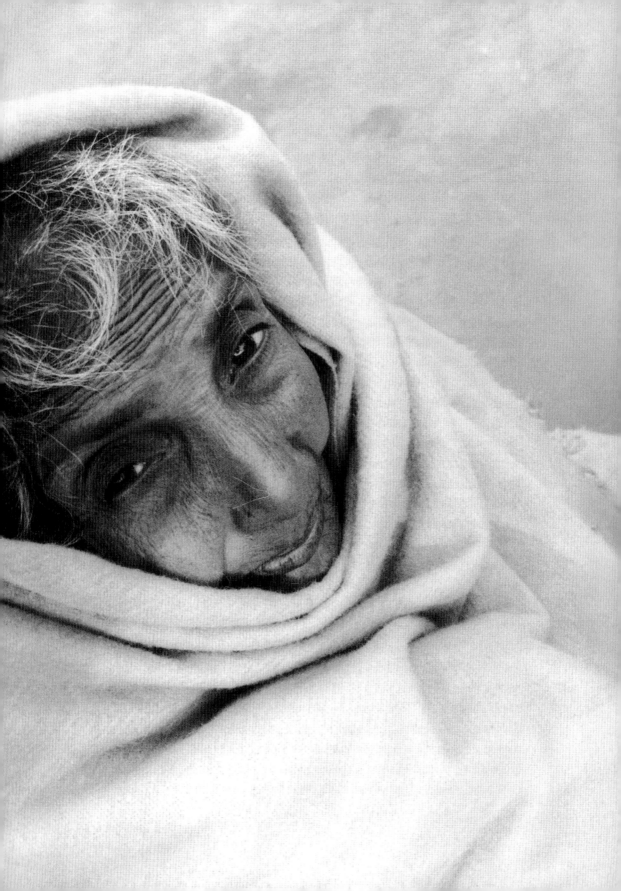

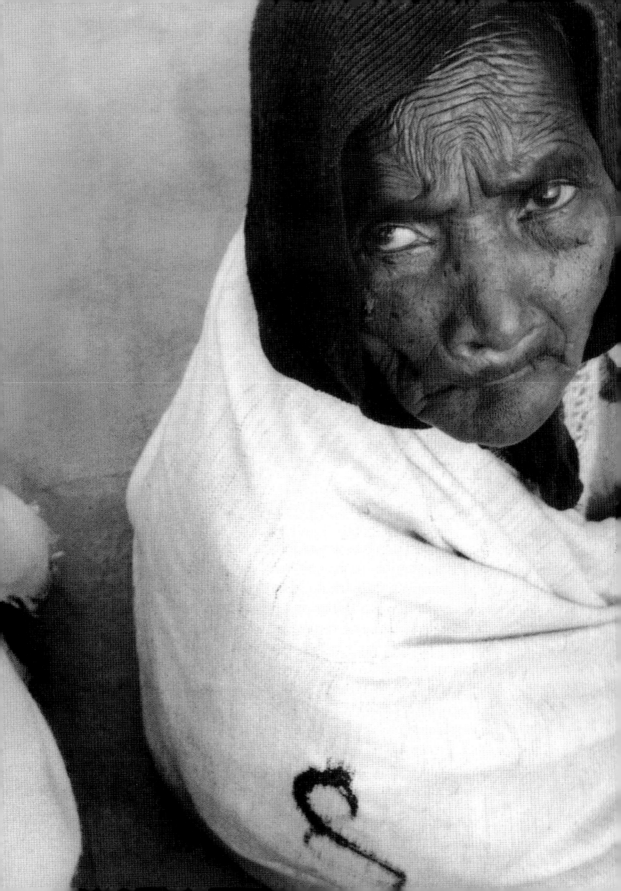

started migrating to the cities in search of jobs, this in turn led to the mushrooming of slums in urban areas with all their attendant consequences – low wages, inadequate jobs, the outbreak of epidemics, crime and much more. Even the First World War was fought for the control of colonies where the industrialised nations like England and Germany could dump their factory-made goods. Besides these colonies supplied raw materials for the industrialised West.

Indian weavers were hit by the East India Company's laws that forced them to sell raw cotton to British traders. No duty was levied on imported goods, while Indian manufactures were heavily taxed. I became a strong advocate of *khadi* [hand spun cotton] after reading Gandhiji's words "every anna spent on *khadi* is so much put into the pockets of a poor and famished" artisan "who would have been without work, and so without food, but for my one anna".

Chaunviyan Shaksiyatan, p. 31 and *Kahaniyan,* pp. 257-260.

SEVEN GREAT DANGERS

The greatest dangers which India faces are, I think, seven:
1. The combination on the one hand of soil erosion, destruction of humus, and leaching out of minerals from the soil, and on the other increasing overpopulation. This combination, if not checked, can result in far greater starvation and impoverishment than has yet been experienced.
2. Violence, including both war and civil strife, physical violence and violence through economic, political, social or religious oppression.
3. Grossly unequal distribution of power as between classes, castes, groups and individuals, between the city and the countryside.
4. Overemphasis on size [giganticism] in organisations,

especially in the realms of politics, finance, industry and commerce.

5. Failure, especially among leaders, to realise that in every realm of activity the means chosen to reach an end must be consistent with the end desired.

6. The prevalent notion amongst the elite that governments or corporations or other large organisations need not obey moral laws recognised as applicable to individuals and others.

7. The loss of faith among leaders and university-educated people in the existence and power of spirituality.

Plant or Perish, p. 2.

EXERCISE

It is not good to lead an idle life. A person can remain healthy only if he is physically active. All humans must walk at least eight miles (fourteen kilometers) every day otherwise they will become victims of high blood pressure, heart problems, diabetes, arthritis, pain in the knees, swollen toes, joint pains and other ailments.

Thoughts and Writings of Bhagat Puran Singhji, p. 71.

His Favourite Verses from Guru Granth Sahib

If one lives in a broken tenement, in tatters
And has neither caste nor status, and wanders alone, in the wilderness,
Has neither friends nor a beloved, nor beauty, nor riches, nor relatives to lean on,
He indeed is the King of the universe if his mind is imbued with the Lord's Name.
One is saved by the dust of His feet, because the Lord is

pleased with him
Guru Granth Sahib, p. 707.

Says Farid, if you long for the Lord
You should be like straw on the floor
Torn by one and trod by another
Only then does one arrive at His door.
Guru Granth Sahib, p. 1378.

He who has enshrined the Name in His heart
He who sees the Lord in every part
He who remembers the Master with every breath
Says Nanak, such a recluse saves the rest.
Guru Granth Sahib, p. 274.

Only by becoming totally detached, and not through mere verbal jargon, can one become a true disciple. One can be such a person only by standing up for truth and by overcoming delusions and fears. The true disciple is...ever busy in the service of the Master. He forgoes hunger, sleep, food and rest. He grinds fresh flour for the free kitchen and fetches water for it as well. He fans the congregation and washes the feet of the Guru. He serves with discipline and is neither woebegone nor flippant. Only thus can he become a devotee at the door of the Lord and get blessed by a shower of love. He will be seen as the first moon of Id, and will emerge a perfect man.
Bhai Gurdas' Var 3, Pauri 18.

END NOTES

INTRODUCTION

p. 8   "was a protection...against starvation...:"
        Raja Ram Shastri, *Social Work Tradition in India*, Welfare Forum and
        Research Organisation, Varanasi, 1966, pp. 6-7.
        "In Islam, spiritual merit has been assigned...:"
        Encyclopaedia of Social Work in India, Publications Division,
        Government of India, New Delhi, 1968, p. 324.
        "Happiness unto him...:" *ibid.*, p. 328.

p. 11   "the secret of religion lay in living...:" *Guru Granth Sahib*, p. 730.

p. 13   "service rendered to humanity...:" Harbans Singh, Editor-in-Chief,
        The Encyclopaedia of Sikhism, Vol. IV, Patiala, 1998, p. 84.
        "*sewa* must be without desire (*nishkam*)...:" *ibid.*, p. 85.
        "In traditional Indian society...:" *ibid.*, p. 84.
        "the pleasure of fanning them [the congregations]...:" *ibid.*, p.85
        "Altruism" it is also pointed out...: Avtar Singh, *Ethics of the Sikhs*,
        Vision and Venture, Patiala, 1970, p. 188.
        "He who is turned towards the Guru...:" Harbans Singh,
        Editor-in-Chief, *The Encyclopaedia of Sikhism*, Vol.IV, p. 84.

1 THE EARLY YEARS

p. 22   "...*itt, rore de utey di*...:" Puran Singh, *Kahaniyan* (in Punjabi).
        A Pingalwara Publication, 2nd ed., Amritsar, 1996, p. 205.
        "My mother would give me a container of corn...:" *ibid.*, pp. 203-04.

p. 28   "My mother was willing to go to any lengths...:" *ibid.*, pp. 229-30.

p. 29   "Once, while going to my village on foot...:" Pritam Singh, 'Bhagat
        Puran Singh', Pingalwara *Souvenir* on Puran Singh's first death
        anniversary, Amritsar, 1994, p. 29.
        "planted in my young mind the seeds of the Sikh faith...:" *ibid.*

p. 32   "*tera put wada aadmi banega*...:" Puran Singh, *Kahaniyan*, p.109.

p. 33   "From it I learnt that the colonial rulers of India...:" "Sikh
        Naujawano! Bhagat Puran Singh de jeewan to Prerna
        Lao,"*Chaunviyan Shaksiyatan* (in Punjabi). A Pingalwara
        Publication, Amritsar, 1998, p.31.

p. 34   "I know I am going to die soon." Puran Singh, *Kahaniyan*, p.116.

2 THE TURNING POINT

p. 37   "The act of carrying Piara Singh on his back...:" Diwan Anand
        Kumar, 'Bhagat Puran Singh and his Pingalwara', *Bhagat Puran
        Singh – A Servant of the People*, A Pingalwara Publication, 1996, p.11.

p. 38   "A tall, shabbily dressed man...:" Bhagat Singh, 'Bhagat Puran
        Singh', *Bhagat Puran Singh - A Servant of the People*, 1996, p.4.

p. 41 "the year 1940 when he [Puran Singh] walked barefoot...:" *ibid.*, p. 5.

p. 44 "for fourteen years before the inception...:"
Diwan Anand Kumar, *ibid.*,p. 11.
"Whatever the work, my willingness to undertake it...:"
Puran Singh, *Kahaniyan*, p.13.
"There was something striking about this tall, gaunt man...:"
Des Raj, in a personal interview, Amritsar, June 1999.
"from Lahore a man who was on his deathbed...:"
Puran Singh, *Kahaniyan*, p.12.

p. 47 "Piara has been the greatest source of strength and inspiration for me...:" *ibid.*, p.26.

p. 48 "Washing filthy clothes with his hands...:" Puran Singh, *Kahaniyan*, pp.262-63. Also see Amrik Singh Bhatia, *Bhagat Puran Singh – The Healer of Agonies*. A Pingalwara Publication, Amritsar, 1997, p.10.

p. 56 "Sometimes his mission appeared quite implausible."
Dr. Daljit Singh, in a personal interview, Amritsar, December 1999.
"No one had his missionary zeal." *ibid.*

3 PINGALWARA

p. 71 "it was always possible that with the project...:"
Puran Singh, *Kahaniyan*, p. 91.
"I want the building to be built...:" *ibid.*

p. 74 "He was seventy years old at that time...:"
Puran Singh, *ibid.*, pp. 36-37.

p. 75 "Mehar Singh, a tenant of Sardar Jaswant Singh Bajaj in Bathinda...:" *Chaunviyan Shaksiyatan*, p.45.
"Pingalwara, as a flower blooming on the tree of Sikh culture...:"
Amrik Singh Bhatia, *Bhagat Puran Singh – The Healer of Agonies*, p. 20.

p. 77 "We had no money in those days for even the basic needs of our patients...:" Chain Masih, in a personal interview, Amritsar, June 1999.

p. 78 "the diligence with which Narain Singh carried out his responsibilities...genuine zeal to serve...:" Puran Singh, *Kahaniyan*, pp. 76-77.
"I have swept the excreta of patients...:"
Pritam Singh, 'Bhagat Puran Singh' Pingalwara *Souvenir*, 1994.

p. 85 "I am an equal claimant...:"
Joginder Singh, in a personal interview, New Delhi, October 1999.

"He felt free to walk into our house...:" *ibid.*

"unending and enormous...were always met generously...:"
Pritam Singh, Pingalwara *Souvenir.*

p. 86 "In our country the helpless and the homeless dying...:"
Bhagat Singh, 'Bhagat Puran Singh', Pingalwara *Souvenir*, pp. 7-8.

"God helps those who help themselves...:"
VN Narayanan, "Humility is my Mace," Pingalwara *Souvenir.*

p. 91 "spectacle of helpless persons dying...:" Bhagat Singh,
'Bhagat Puran Singh', p. 8.

"Such an idea could only take birth in the mind...:" *ibid.*, pp. 6-7.

"a rich person always thinks of endowing...:" *ibid.*, p. 7.

"is not another...hospital, but greater boarding facilities...:" *ibid.*

"at least here I will die in peace and comfort." Puran Singh,
Kahaniyan, p.116.

p. 92 "Mine has been a full and meaningful life...:"
Pritam Singh, Pingalwara *Souvenir.*

p. 93 "I do not even know how to thank the Gurdwaras...:" *ibid.*

p. 94 "I have no personal demands...:" Pritam Singh,
Pingalwara *Souvenir.*

p. 100 "He asked me if I could persuade the Reserve Bank of India...:"
Khushwant Singh, 'Samaritan of Amritsar', *Bhagat Puran Singh –
A Servant of the People*, 1996, p.32.

"as with many other good people he has a kink in him...:" *ibid.*

"I consider him one of the best-read persons in Amritsar...:"
Dr. Daljit Singh, in a personal interview, Amritsar, December 1999.

p. 105 "the immense pleasure and satisfaction I got...:"
Puran Singh, *Kahaniyan*, p.203.

4 THE TRANSCENDENT SPIRIT

p. 119 "aware in 1928 that the denudation of forests...:"
Puran Singh, *Peril of Survival*, A Pingalwara Publication,
Amritsar, 1998, p.4.

p. 120 "painfully aware of a vital change in...:" *ibid.*, pp. 67-68.

"If the ministers who sit comfortably in New Delhi...:"
Mira Behn, 'Controlling Floods' *ibid.*, p. 27.

"They tell one the oak cannot grow on such steep slopes...:"
Mira Behn, 'Vanishing Oaks', *ibid.*, pp. 22-23.

p. 122 "I took to heart the warnings of Mira Behn...:"
Puran Singh, *ibid.*, p. 5.

"It was in 1963 that I reported in an article published...:"
Sunderlal Bahuguna, *What the Trees Mean to the Villages*,

A Pingalwara Publication, 1996, p. 3.
p. 124 "when the sports goods company was allotted *ash* trees...:"
ibid.,p. 5.
"village women led by Gaura Devi...:" *ibid.*, p. 5.
"She was overjoyed when she heard...:"
Quoted by Sunderlal Bahuguna in *Peril of Survival*, p. 71.
p. 125 "preparedness to immediately yoke myself tirelessly...:"
Puran Singh, *ibid.*, p.18.
"great and ancient civilizations from the valleys of the Nile...:"
Partap Singh, 'Trees - Benefactors of Mankind', *ibid.*, p. 11.
"These civilizations were destroyed...:" *ibid.*
p. 126 "The bitter lesson which must be learnt...:" *ibid.*
"In our own Punjab state...:" *ibid.*, p. 12.
"the profiles of soil exposed...:" *ibid.*
"live sand dunes can be seen...:" *ibid.*, p. 13.
"Planting of trees...is described in India's ancient texts...:"
Puran Singh, *Kahaniyan*, p. 202.
p. 127 "My mother had planted three trees side by side...:" *ibid.*
"the green forest cover in India...:"
Puran Singh, *Plant or Perish*, A Pingalwara Publication, Amritsar,
1999, p. 1.
p. 130 "he would insist you should come...:"
Dr. Madanjit Kaur, in a personal interview, Amritsar, November
1999.
"If you respect me, come to me walking...:"
SS Rahi, in a personal interview, Amritsar, November 1999.
p. 131 "Sometimes he would be stranded at the railway crossing...:"
Mohinder Singh Bal in a personal interview, Amritsar, November
1999.
"all great teachers were walkers...:"
Khushwant Singh, *Bhagat Puran Singh – A Servant of the People*,
p. 31.
p. 132 "a pathfinder who warned ordinary men and women...:"
Dr. Inderjit Kaur, in a personal interview, Amritsar, June 1999.
"Bhagatji regarded the earth as a holy shrine...:" *ibid.*
"*Pawan guru pani pita mata dharat mahat...:*"
Guru Granth Sahib, p. 8.
"pure water and clean air being the byproducts of forests...:"
'Need to Conserve Water', *The Hindu*, 4 June, 1988.
A Pingalwara Reprint, Amritsar, 1988, pp. 14-15.
"austere use of water; alternatives to minimise...:" *ibid.*

p.134 "Poverty in India will grow if the emphasis...:"
Shankar Ranganathan, 'Population: The Neglected Factor,'
Vaigyanik (Hindi), January-June, 1981, A Pingalwara Reprint,
Amritsar, 1983, p. 7.

p.135 "When God created man and woman...:" Puran Singh, *Jatti-Satti*
(in Punjabi), A Pingalwara Publication, Amritsar, 1982, p. 80.
"There is nothing wrong with marriage...:" *ibid.*, pp. 80-81.

p. 136 "She embodies in herself compassion and love of humanity...:"
Eileen Egan, *Mother Teresa – The Spirit and the Work*,
Sidgwick & Jackson, London, 1985, p. 398.

p. 137 "who had literally built Pingalwara...:" Puran Singh,
Be-ghar Jawaan Istri (in Punjabi), A Pingalwara Publication,
Amritsar, 1999.
"Given Bhagat Puran Singh's outstanding devotion...:"
Amrit Kaur, 'A Farewell to Bhagat Puran Singh',
The Sikh Review, Vol.40, No. 11, Calcutta, November, 1992, p. 51.
"We respectfully submit that at times of hardships...:" *ibid.*

p. 138 "*Bibi, wapis ja ke*...:" Bibi Avinash Kaur Kang, in a telephone
conversation from Brampton, Ontario, Canada, January 2000.

p.144 "The ominous moment came to pass...:"
Amrik Singh Bhatia, *The Healer of Agonies*, pp. 27-28.

INDEX